Welcome to
OTTUMWA
1896

Cover illustration: From a postcard view, taken about 1900, showing East Main Street from the intersection of Court and Main. Most of the buildings at left (north side of Main Street) remain today. Buildings to the right (south side of Main Street) were removed in the 1970s and replaced by the Wapello Building.
Kerfoots Clothing store was located at 103-105 East Main Street. Though a streetcar system was operating in Ottumwa by the time this photo was taken, tracks were not yet laid on this block of Main Street, which was still unpaved when this photo was taken.

Back cover inset: A reproduction of the restored color version of the original cover of the Souvenir Book, as published by the Ottumwa *Daily Democrat* in 1896.

Welcome to
OTTUMWA
1896

Second Regiment
Iowa National Guard
Annual Encampment
Ottumwa, Iowa
July 25 to August 1, 1896

Souvenir Book
originally published in 1896
by the Ottumwa *Daily Democrat*

PBL Limited
Ottumwa, Iowa

Copyright 2019 by Leigh Michaels

Cover and design copyright 2019 PBL Limited

Original edition published 1896 by the Ottumwa Daily Democrat
Reprint edition published 2013
Expanded edition published 2019

10 9 8 7 6 5 4 3 2 1

ISBN 1-892689-97-9
ISBN 13: 978-1-892689-97-9

Printed in the United States of America

Illustrations: Cover & page 2, courtesy of Paul Anderson. Pages 108, 118, 136, 138 courtesy of the Lemberger Collection.

All rights reserved. Except for brief passages quoted in any review, the reproduction or utilization of this work in whole or in part, in any form or by any electronic, mechanical, or other means, now known or hereinafter invented, including xerography, photocopying and recording, or in any information storage and retrieval system, is forbidden without the express permission of the publisher. For permission contact:
 Rights Editor
 PBL Limited
 P.O. Box 935
 Ottumwa IA 52501-0935
 www.pbllimited.com

This book is dedicated
to all who have served
and are serving today
in our nation's defense

Welcome to Ottumwa 1896

The original cover, restored as much as possible from its faded and badly-damaged condition. The illustration was in color. The cover of the book was pasteboard and the binding was a tied cord, visible at left.

Contents

Introduction
9

About the Encampment
10-11

The Souvenir Book
12-63

The Ottumwa *Daily Democrat*
and the encampment
64-79

Ottumwa in 1896
80-124

The world in 1896
125-133

History of The Second Regiment,
Iowa National Guard
134-143

Sources
144

Welcome to Ottumwa 1896

The original cover, before restoration

Introduction

In 1896, the Second Regiment of the Iowa National Guard held its annual encampment in Ottumwa, Iowa, the hometown of Company G, one of twelve companies which made up the regiment. One of the town's newspapers, the Ottumwa *Daily Democrat*, produced a souvenir book for the national guardsmen. The 50-page book included information about the guard regiment and the town, much of which appears in no other local publication. The choice of subject matter -- which businesses and persons to include -- suggests that people and businesses who helped to sponsor the publication were more likely to appear in its pages.

Only a few copies have survived. This edition is produced from a badly-damaged original. Each page was scanned and individually restored. Some text could not be salvaged, but where possible it has been deciphered and reset. Recovered text has been added directly on the page, where space allowed, or on a facing page.

Supplemental text has also been added to the facsimile pages, especially in photo cutlines when street addresses were not included in the original. Information added to the text came mainly from two city directories: the 1894-95 Directory of the City of Ottumwa and Wapello County, published in 1894 by Ottumwa Blank Book & Printing Company, Ottumwa, and the 1897-1898 Ottumwa City Directory produced by W. H. McCoy. Added information is reproduced as it appears in the directories. Because not all locations had been assigned numbers at the time, sometimes the directory identified houses by the nearest intersection and businesses by the building in which they were located.

It is important to note that the street addresses in the 1896 Souvenir Book or in the directories may not match today's numbering system, since the organization of Ottumwa street addresses was changed in 1911.

In addition to reproducing the original pages of the Souvenir Book, sections have been added about the National Guard unit's history from its inception through the first World War, as well as the city, the newspaper which produced the book, and world events of the time.

The Ottumwa Public Library was instrumental in obtaining microfilm of the Ottumwa *Daily Democrat* from 1896, including the eight days in which the Second Regiment was in town, from the Iowa State Historical Library. The Ottumwa Public Library is also the source of the city directory information.

We hope you will enjoy revisiting the Ottumwa of 1896.

Welcome to Ottumwa 1896

About the Encampment

Right: Story about the involvement of Chariton's Company H in the National Guard encampment planned for Ottumwa, as reprinted in the Ottumwa *Daily Democrat.* The company traveled from Chariton to Ottumwa by train

Far right: From the Ottumwa *Sunday Democrat* front page, Sunday, July 19, 1896, giving details about the upcoming encampment

The Encampment.

Co. H has received orders and will go into camp at Camp Cloutman, Ottumwa, Iowa, leaving Chariton Saturday morning at 8:30. The boys will be away one week, returning the following Saturday. This year it is a regimental encampment and twelve companies will do duty and study military tactics at Camp Cloutman. The twelve companies are from Keokuk, Davenport, Washington, Centerville, Ft. Madison, Ottumwa, Chariton, Iowa City, Grinnell, Newton and Tipton. Lieut. Col. Jackson, of Muscatine, is regimental commander. A governor's reception and ball will be given by the Wapello Club, of Ottumwa, on Tuesday evening and will no doubt be one of the leading social fetures of the week. Quite a number of Chariton people have signified their intention of attending the encampment part of the week. The company will leave here with forty enlisted men and three commissioned officers, being the same number enlisted for camp duty at Centerville last year. Several applications were filed, but the state only furnishes equipments for forty enlisted men. A special baggage car and coach has been assigned the company, and the same will be attached to No. 10.
—Chariton Democrat.

Second Regiment Iowa National Guard

THE ENCAMPMENT.

Programme of Exercises for the Boys in Blue.

The encampment of the Second regiment, I. N. G., will begin at camp Cloutman, adjoining the South Side ball park, next Saturday.

The programme has not yet been completed, but the following is about the routine for each day:

Reveille, 5:30 a. m.
Roll call, 5:45 a. m.
Divine service, 6:00 a. m.
Breakfast, 6:30 a. m.
Guard Mount, 8:00 a. m.
Company drill, 9:00 a. m.
Battallion drill, 10 a. m.
Dinner, 12.
Battalion or regimental drill, 2 p. m.
Supper, 6:00 p. m.
Dress parade, 7:00 p. m.

It will be seen that the first drill is at eight o'clock. This will last until about 8:30, and is one of the best drills of the day. Company drill at 9 will last about forty-five minutes, and battallion at 10 will last until 11:30, thus keeping the boys hustling pretty lively until dinner time. The commanding officer, it is understood, is thinking seriously of having no drills at all in the afternoon, and at the most there will but one mentioned in the above programme. This will be good news for the members of the militia, their experience at former camps being yet fresh in their minds. Of long drills under a sun that was almost unbearable, and under the oppressive heat of which many were prostrated. The programme as published above is subject to change and after guard mount may be entirely transposed.

Dress parade in the evening will probably be witnessed by more spectators than any other drill.

As signified by the name it will be in full dress suit and helmet and makes a nice drill. Probably the drill giving one or more distinct ideas of the work of the army in the field is the regimental drill. It is very interesting to watch and gives one a good idea of how an army looks when in action.

The officers of the Second regiment who will have charge of the encampment here are Col. Guest, of Burlington, Lieut. Col. Jackson of Muscatine, Maj. Lambert of Newton, Major Moffett of Tipton, Major Glasgow of Washington, and Capt. Goedeke of Burlington, regimental adjutant. Inspector of small arms practice is Capt. Kemble of Muscatine. The chaplain is R. C. McIlwain of Keokuk, quartermaster, H. J. Huiskamp of Burlington; engineer and signal officer, C. R. Fickes of Iowa City; commissary, Chas. Wilson of Washington; surgeon, C. M. Robertson, Davenport; assistant surgeon, J. W. Harriman, Iowa City.

Arrangements are all completed for the reception of Governor Drake at the rooms of the Wapello club on Tuesday evening, July 28. The reception committee has been completed and consists of the following well known Ottumwa men:

Maj. W. C. Wyman, Maj. Samuel Mahon, A. W. Lee, Capt. George H. Wheelock, Capt. D. A. Emery, R. H. Moore, Calvin Manning, Hon. H. L. Waterman, E. M. B. Scott, Capt. J. G. Hutchison, Hon. J. H. Merrill, J. W. Garner, F. W. Simmons, E. M. Jenison, Capt. S. H. Harper, R. L. Tilton J. D. Ferree, Co. G, I. N. G.

Welcome to Ottumwa 1896

The Souvenir Booklet

THE SOUVENIR BOOKS.

Today the distribution of a copy of THE DEMOCRAT Souvenir Book was made to each soldier of the regiment. The books were given out through Co. G's headquarters, the captain of each visiting company being presented with a copy for each of his men. The boys appreciated the gift and gave three cheers for the local company and THE DEMOCRAT.

A HOT DRESS PARADE.

The dress parade given last evening about 7 o'clock proved to be a hot one for the short time it took to complete

Above: Notice on the front page of the *Daily Democrat* of July 31, 1896, regarding the Souvenir Book.

Ottumwa Daily Democrat

SOUVENIR

...OF THE...

2nd Regiment Encampment

I. N. G.

Ottumwa, Iowa, July 25 to Aug. 1, 1896

CONTAINING NUMEROUS HALF-TONE ILLUSTRATIONS PERTINENT TO THE OCCASION AND REFLECTIVE OF THE CITY OF OTTUMWA

Compiled by
HAMILTON KIRK WATKINS

Press of
GEORGE H. SIMMONDS

Previous page: Original title page. *"Containing numerous half-tone illustrations..."* *Half-tone* is a method of reproducing photographs using just one color of ink (black) in the form of dots, by varying the size and spacing of the dots to create an image which the human eye blends together into smooth continuous tones. A screen is used to break the photographic image into dots which a standard letterpress or offset press can reproduce.
The technique, still used in most newspapers and print media, was relatively new when the Souvenir Book was published. (The first printed photograph was published in 1873.) Prior to the invention of half-tone technology, newspapers used photographs only as source material. Artists made etchings or sketches -- line drawings -- which could be reproduced on the newspaper's press. Since photographs were still tedious to process in 1896, line drawings were still used in many illustrations and ads.

A. E. Woollett, Official Photographer for this Souvenir

The Only Up-to-Date Photographer in Ottumwa, Iowa.

WOOLLETT & KROEGER

DEALERS IN

Pianos, Organs and All Musical Merchandise

South Market, Near Main Street

Ottumwa, Iowa

Alfred E. Woollett, photographer, 208 S. Market

HON. FRANCIS MARION DRAKE
Governor of Iowa
Commander-in-Chief Iowa National Guard

    Francis Marion Drake, born in Illinois in 1830, later moved to Centerville, Iowa where his name is still prominent.
    In the 1850s, during the Gold Rush, he led expeditions from Iowa to California. During the Civil War he achieved the rank of brevet brigadier general and was involved in numerous battles including Marks Mills in 1864. Drake was wounded there and taken prisoner, though he was later paroled; 1,200 of his troops were taken prisoner by the Confederates and held at Camp Ford in Tyler, Texas.

Introductory.

ON the armory of the commonwealth of Venice is this inscription:

"Happy is that city which in
time of war thinks of peace."

Appropos of this present time, while the gallant Second Regiment is encamped within our midst with all the trophies and trappings of war, is the presentation to each soldier and officer of a copy of this Souvenir, serving as a memento of the Encampment and reflective of the city of Ottumwa.

On behalf of the citizens of Ottumwa a hearty welcome is extended to all the soldier boys and officers present.

Yours truly,
THE OTTUMWA DEMOCRAT,
Co. G., 2nd REG'T., I. N. G.

After the Civil War, he practiced criminal law for about six years, then worked in railroads and as a banker, organizing the Centerville National Bank where he was president until his death in 1903.

In 1895 he was nominated by the Republican Party for governor of Iowa, was elected in November 1895, and served from 1896 through 1898.

He founded and endowed Drake University, located in Des Moines, Iowa, and the university is named after him.

Roster of Officers
OF THE
Second Regiment, Infantry, I. N. G.

Colonel—
    James A. Guest.

Lieutenant-Colonel—
    Douglas V. Jackson.

Majors—
    Elliott E. Lambert.
    John T. Moffit.

Regimental Adjutant—Captain—
    Frederick Goedecke.

Batalion Adjutants—First Lieut's—
    John A. Dunlap.
    James C. France.
    Frank W. Bishop.

Inspector Small Arms Practice—Captain—
    Charles W. Kemble.

Quartermaster—First Lieut.—
    Herman J. Huiskamp, Jr.

Commissary—First Lieut.—
    Charles J. Wilson.

Engineer and Signal Officer—First Lieut.—
    Claude Sweinhart.

Surgeon—Major—
    Charles M. Robertson.

Assistant Surgeon—Captain—
    John W. Harriman.

Additional Ass't Surgeon—First Lieut.—
    Frank C. Roberts.

Chaplain—Captain—
    E. C. McIlwain.

COMPANY A.
Capt., Sumner T. Bisbee.
1st Lieut., Frank M. Fuller.
2nd Lieut., Thos. H. R. Robins.

COMPANY B.
Capt., Ober ?. Pough.
1st Lieut., ?
2nd Lieut., ?

COMPANY C.
Capt., John Tillie.
1st Lieut., ...
2nd Lieut., ...

COMPANY D.
Capt., ... L. Glasgow.
1st Lieut., Wm. H. Pulton.
2nd Lieut., ?. W. Harvey.

COMPANY E.
Capt., ...
1st Lieut., ...
2nd Lieut., Oscar M. Cole.

COMPANY F.
Capt., George P. Anthes.
1st Lieut., ?rd C. Chambers.
2nd Lieut., ?erbert Davis.

COMPANY G.
Capt., Harry H. Caughlan.
1st Lieut., Frank W. Eckers.
2nd Lieut., Chas. S. Tindell.

COMPANY H.
Capt., Harry O. Penier.
1st Lieut., Will B. Barger.
2nd Lieut., George E. Whitlock.

COMPANY I.
Capt., Wm. H. Goodrell.
1st Lieut., Eugene F. T. Cherry.
2nd Lieut., Leigh A. Stocking.

COMPANY K.
Capt., Arthur C. Norris.
1st Lieut., ...
2nd Lieut., Burdette A. Abel.

COMPANY L.
Capt., Chas. H. Rinehart.
1st Lieut., Henry T. Kennedy.
2nd Lieut., Wm. E. McMurray.

COMPANY M.
Capt., Lewis J. Rowell.
1st Lieut., ...
2nd Lieut., Frank H. Gunsolus.

MAJ. WM. G. WYMAN
Military Sec'y to Gov. Drake

LT.-COL. FRANK P. CLARKSON
Aid-de-Camp to Gov. Drake

GEN. H. H. WRIGHT
Adjutant-General of Iowa

Left: **Company B**
Capt., Robert T. French (?)
1st Lieut., T-- (illegible) C. Dale (?)
2nd Lieut., Jacob H. M--er (illegible)

GEN. JAMES T. PRIESTLEY
Surgeon-General of Iowa

GEN. JOHN R. PRIME
Adjt.-Gen. under Gov. Jackson

The Iowa National Guard.

WHAT a tribute to the Republican form of Government is the fact that this great and glorious Union of ours stands upright and firm, "a government of the people, for the people, and by the people," and not a government, which, but for its millions of glittering bayonets and thousands of cannon would soon crumble and decay. The combined standing armies of Great Britain, Germany and Russia numbers 17,376,865 men and all of the crowned heads of Europe are constantly advocating measures for the increasing of the armies and navies of their respective governments. The standing army of the United States numbers only 28,000.

It is true that the rapid growth of this government and the liability of its becoming involved in a difficulty with some foreign power has made necessary the increase of our navy, still no increase in our standing army has been made. The main reason of this is the excellent and patriotic National Guard, of which every state in the Union is proud. In all the difficulties which of late years have demanded the presence of troops to maintain the dignity of our laws, the National Guard has proved efficient. Every state in the Union has recognized the necessity of a well-disciplined state militia, and, while appropriations by the Iowa state legislature, to assist in maintaining the guard, have, as a rule, been very meagre, the ardor and patriotism of its members, who have spent, not only their time, but money, has brought it to a very high standard of excellence. Many of the companies of the Iowa National Guard spend more money for armory rent alone, than is given them by state appropriation. The Seventeenth General Assembly of Iowa passed a law in March, 1878, providing for the organization of the "Iowa National Guard" and what was formerly known as the State Militia, was merged into that organization. Since that time the succeeding sessions of the state legislature have passed bills effecting the regulation of the guard. April 30, 1892, the guard was reorganized under the new military law, by transforming the six eight-company regiments into four batalion regiments of twelve companies each. The present numerical strength of the guard is 2,274 enlisted men and officers. Made up as it is, of the young manhood of Iowa, the National Guard contains the best brain, brawn and patriotic spirit to be found the world over. Many of its members are men of the most rigid athletic training. It numbers among its officers many of the veterans of 1861-5, those who were tried and true on the actual field of battle, and who have a correct conception of the dignity and duties which will maintain that standard of efficiency and discipline which will make the guard of the highest value in answering the shortest call of its state or country.

THE SECOND REGIMENT

Among the regiments of the Iowa National Guard none stand higher than the gallant Second, which it has been a pleasure to the citizens of Ottumwa to welcome on this occasion. A roster of the officers of this regiment is found elsewhere herein, and in point of inspections, the Second Regiment stands as high as any in the state. The record of this regiment, in active service, at the call of the state, is given as follows:

1879. Company A, Second Regiment, Fairfield, Capt. W. A. Daggett; ordered to guard jail and protect prisoner threatened by mob.

1883. Company E, Second Regiment, Centerville, Capt. J. T. Connor; ordered out to disperse mob and protect railroad property.

1884. Aug. 20. Company B, Second Regiment, Davenport, Capt. E. I. Cameron; Company C, Second Regiment, Muscatine, Capt. F. Welker; warned to be ready for duty, in anticipation of violence from striking miners at What Cheer, Keokuk county.

1885. Company E, Second Regiment, Centerville, Capt. J. T. Connor; ordered by sheriff of Appanoose county to disperse mob organized to lynch prisoner.

1887. August 9. Company C, Second Regiment, Muscatine, Capt. C. F. Garlock; ordered to oust proprietors of saloons established contrary to law, adjoining camp of First Brigade.

During the trouble in May, 1894, when the workmen from neighboring mines, who were on a strike, concentrated at Evans to force the white miners out, in order that the entire force might unite in an attack on the colored miners at Muchakinock, the governor was appealed to for assistance. The Evans miners refused to go out and the strikers annoyed them as they passed to and from their work. Adjutant-General Prime went in person to the scene of disorder, and by his cool judgment and decision averted what might have been a bloody battle, for the colored miners would not have hesitated to defend themselves. On May 30, 1894, General Prime called out Companies A, H and F, of the Third Regiment. Under command of Major Loper they were placed at Evans to protect the working miners. Companies G and K of the second Regiment, also called out, were stationed at Muchakinock. General Prime said if the miners at Evans and Muchakinock wanted to work, he would see they were not disturbed. He was as good as his word. The appearance of the troops at once restored order, not a gun was fired, and what, with less judicious management, might have resulted in a deadly conflict was settled without bloodshed. In addition to the service rendered by the Second Regiment to the State, every regiment of the Iowa National Guard has at some time or other since its organization been called out and rendered efficient service on occasions similar to those in which the Second Regiment was used.

COL. JAS. A. GUEST.

SECOND REGIMENT OFFICERS.

1. Capt. Fred C. Goedecke, Adjt., Burlington. 2. Maj. John T. Moffit, Tipton. 3. Capt. James D. Glasgow, Co. D. Washington. 4. Capt. A. C. Norris, Co. K. Grinnell. 5. Col. James A. Guest, Commander, Burlington. 6. Lt.-Col. Douglas V. Jackson, Muscatine. 7. Capt. John Tillie, Co. C. Muscatine. 8. Capt. W. H. Ogle, Co. E. Centerville.

Company G., 2nd Regiment, I. N. G.

CAPT. H. H. CAUGHLAN
Present Capt. Co. G.

THE history of Co. G., 2nd Regiment, I. N. G., which has long been the pride of the citizens of Ottumwa, dates back to April 19, 1884, when it was duly sworn in by W. C. Wyman as mustering officer. The first election of officers resulted in H. L. Hedrick being elected captain, W. C. Wyman, 1st Lieut., and C. K. Blake, 2nd Lieut. The boys exhibited much enthusiasm, and at once secured the old M. E. Church as an armory. This building stood on a portion of the cite of the present Wapello county court house, and is illustrated elsewhere herein. They occupied this building until 1892, when they secured more suitable quarters in the Grand Opera House building, where the armory is now located. The company did not attend the regimental encampment of 1884 on account of not having received their uniforms. The first camp experience of the company was in 1885 at Centerville, Col. H. H. Wright, now Adjutant-General of Iowa, being the colonel in command. The following is a list of commissioned officers of the company since its organization:

Captains—H. L. Hedrick, W. A. McGrew, Geo. H. Wheelock, D. A. Emery, H. H. Caughlan.

1st Lieutenants—W. C. Wyman, C. K. Blake, G. H. Wheelock, D. A. Emery, A. N. Barnes, H. H. Caughlan, F. W. Eckers.

2nd Lieutenants—C. K. Blake, G. H. Wheelock, H. F. Field, D. A. Emery, J. B. McCarroll, W. T. Harper, Jr., D. T. Miller, J. T. Emerson, J. W. Soale, F. W. Eckers, C. S. Tindell.

LIST OF ENCAMPMENTS ATTENDED BY CO. G.

Regimental Encampment		Centerville, 1885
Brigade	"	Oscaloosa, 1886
Brigade	"	Ottumwa, 1887
Regimental	"	Barlington, 1888
Regimental	"	Ft. Madison, 1889
Brigade	"	Des Moines, 1890
Regimental	"	Davenport, 1891
Regimental	"	Barlington, 1894
Brigade	"	Centerville, 1895

Camped at dedication of World's Columbian Exposition, October, 1892.

Camped at Inauguration Governor Boies at Des Moines, Feby., 1890.

Camped at Muchakinock in May, 1894, when trouble was expected on account of a strike of the coal miners.

Co. G., during its long and successful career, maintained a standing above the average at various inspections, and while it has never posed as a "crack" company, it has always held the reputation of being a good serviceable company, and the people of Ottumwa are proud of it. It has contained in the past, as at present, the flower of the youth of this city, and should necessity demand it, which God forbid, Co. G. will acquit itself with honor when called upon to face the enemy in defense of its country's flag.

/////////

CAPT. D. A. EMERY
Formerly Capt. Co. G.

Wapello County Court House

THE OLD CO. G. ARMORY
Formerly the M. E. Church.

THIS magnificent structure, illustrated below, which was erected at a cost of $120,000, is one of the finest public buildings of its kind to be found in any city of the west. The superstructure is built of gray sandstone and the entire building is fire proof. Its interior finish and appointments are of the best and the citizens of Ottumwa and Wapello county are proud of it. The court house is located at the northwest corner of Court and Fourth streets. It faces a very pretty city park, a portion of which is shown in the illustration. The bird's eye view from the tower of the court house is a treat which the eye is seldom offered. For miles and miles the rich and rolling surrounding country stretches out, and forms a scenic picture long to be remembered by the lover of nature. Winding its way peacefully through the valley, flows the beautiful Des Moines river.

The Old Armory

ABOVE is a picture of the old Co. G. armory which was occupied by the company from its organization in 1884 to 1892, when the present armory in the Opera House block was occupied. This building was for years the M. E. Church, and occupied what is now the west portion of the Wapello county court house site. The picture shows Co. G. drawn up in front of the armory.

WAPELLO COUNTY COURT HOUSE

"Our Mess"

Grouping for a Picture

"Off Duty"

The City of Ottumwa, Iowa

"The Lowell of the West."

RICH in the historic lore for which the region is so famous, this city very fittingly derives its name from a tribe of Indians of which Appanoose was the chief. He was known as the "Lone Chief," because he persisted in refusing the invitation of Chief Wapello and others to leave his camp on the site of what is now the city of Ottumwa, and join Wapello's tribe. It is said that "Ottumwanoc" means the "place of perseverance or self-will," which the Indians applied to the home of Appanoose and his tribe, because of their determination to remain there. The world-wide reputation of Ottumwa as a pushing, progressive city, whose population is ever up and doing, is sufficiently established to need no extended mention here. All of its business interests are solid and the men behind them of that energetic truly American spirit which surmounts all obstacles and wins success in matters both great and small. Numbered among its citizens are some of those hardy pioneers who were the early white settlers of the state. It is not our purpose to go into the history of Ottumwa here, but to briefly mention the city as it exists to-day.

Located as it is, in the center of the richest of the coal mining and farming portion of Iowa, the city of Ottumwa is the hub of a fifty-mile circle, within which reside 400,000 people. From this territory Ottumwa draws the greatest portion of its trade in the retail line, but the product of its factories finds markets the world over, and its jobbing houses cover this and surrounding states. In shipping facilities Ottumwa has advantages which are offered by few cities in the state. Six great railroads pass through the city, bringing it in close commercial relations with the following countries:

DR. D. A. LA FORCE,
Mayor.

C., M. & St. P. R'y—Iowa, Keokuk, Wapello, Appanoose and Wayne, in Iowa, and Putnam, Sullivan, Grundy and Livingston in Missouri, embracing a population of 161,828.

C., B. & Q. R'y—Henry, Jefferson, Wapello, Monroe, Lucas, Clark, Union, Wayne and Decatur in Iowa, and Harrison in Missouri, a population of 174,553.

Chicago, Rock Island & Pacific—Marion, Mahaska, Wapello, Van Buren, Davis, Appanoose, Jefferson, Washington and Wayne in Iowa, and Mercer, Grundy and Davies in Missouri, with a population of 245,996.

Wabash—Marion, Mahaska, Wapello, Davis, Van Buren and Appanoose in Iowa, and Schuyler, Adair, Macon, Randolph, Boone, Putnam, Sullivan, Linn and Carroll in Missouri, a population of 327,166.

Iowa Central—Jasper, Poweshiek, Mahaska and Wapello, with 102,568.

Chicago, Fort Madison & Des Moines—Wapello, Jefferson, Van Buren, Lee and Henry, with 80,758.

Roster of City Officials

Mayor	D. A. La Force	Police Judge	Charles Hall
City Treasurer	S. L. Vest	Chief of Police	B. W. Van Der Veer
City Auditor	L. M. Godley	City Marshal	Michael Morrissey
City Clerk	L. M. Godley	Sidewalk Comm'r	Eber Dixon
City Solicitor	W. W. Epps	City Physician	L. J. Baker, M. D.
City Engineer	C. R. Allen	Police Captain	Daniel Hannon

Common Council

President, pro tem	S. D. Baker	Third Ward	Claude Myers
Aldermen-at-Large	L. E. Rogers / S. A. Spilman	Fourth Ward	C. W. Major
First Ward	T. F. Keefe	Fifth Ward	H. D. Crawford
Second Ward	S. D. Baker	Sixth Ward	Sanford Withrow

The city of Ottumwa has made rapid progress in the past few years in the matter of public improvements, among the most important of which has been the adoption of brick paving. Nearly all of the principal thoroughfares are now paved with brick which are manufactured at home. Its public school system is not surpassed in the state, and stands high in the estimation of all. The roster of city officials who are in charge of its various departments, is given above. The waterworks system and lighting plant are touched on elsewhere.

GRAND OPERA HOUSE.
The Present Armory of Co. G. is Located in this Building.
Main and Jefferson Streets. The building's first level became Market on Main

CLAUDE M. MYERS
Alderman Third Ward

J. D. STEVENS
Chief of Fire Department

B. W. VAN DER VEER
Chief of Police

G. J. GARRIOTT
Deputy County Clerk

W. R. WARREN
County Treasurer

W. B. Wycoff residence
179 E. Court
William B. Wycoff sold real estate

Left: Samuel Mahon was born in Ireland in 1840 and moved with his family to Xenia, Ohio, in 1849. He worked on the family farm and in a retail store until 1861, when he enlisted as first lieutenant of the Seventh Iowa Infantry, where he served until the close of the war. He was promoted to major in 1864. Serving in all of the campaigns under Generals Grant and Sherman in the west, he was also with General Sherman on his march from Atlanta to the sea. Following the war, Mahon joined the firm of J.H. Merrill & Co., dealing in wholesale groceries, and was affiliated with Morey Clay Products Co. as well as with several banks.

Samuel Mahon's residence was at 140 E. Court

Dr. S. E. O'Neill residence
445 N. Market
Dr. O'Neill's office was in the Hofmann Block at Market and Second Streets

T.D. Foster residence, Market and Fifth Streets
Thomas Dove Foster was manager of John Morrell & Company

T. J. Phillips residence
Putnam near Gara
Thomas J. Phillips was assistant
superintendent of Whitebreast Fuel Co.

Major Wm. C. Wyman
residence, 407 N. Court
Major in the 2nd Regiment ING
associated with J. Prugh & Co.
(crockery & glassware)

Wm. Daggett residence
105 W. Fifth
William Daggett was
vice president
of Iowa National Bank

John B. Dennis residence
329 W. Fifth
John B. Dennis was associated
with Samuel T. Lilburn & Co.,
selling butter and eggs

RESIDENCE OF JOHN B DENNIS

The original Hofmann Block, built in 1893 at the corner of Market and Second Streets, by Bernard Hofmann. This building was destroyed by fire in March 1940 and was replaced by the current Hofmann Building.

Wm. Daggett, President   Arthur Gephart, Treasurer   Wm. McNett, Attorney   B. L. Hoge, Secretary

Equitable Loan Company

Ottumwa and Des Moines, Iowa

Capital $2,000,000; Guarantee Capital $200,000

AMONG the financial institutions of Ottumwa, the Equitable Loan Company stands high. The growth of this company's business has been rapid and fast increasing. It is the only company in the state that absolutely guarantees the date of maturity of its stock. It guarantees a profit of eleven per cent. on "prepaid stock" and is a safe and profitable investment for parties having money to invest in amounts of $100.00 and over. The company invite an investigation of this stock by any one having money to invest.

One of the strong features of this institution is the fact that it has one-half of its assets invested in first real estate farm mortgages which alone should insure to the investing public that the institution is conducting its business on a safe basis. Its books and affairs are examined once each year by the state auditor. Its officers are required to give a bond and deposit same with the state auditor.

In financial circles this company is regarded as one of the leading institutions of its kind in the state, and the gentlemen who are at its head are all time-tried men of affairs whose business ability and sound judgement have won for them a high place in the estimation of all.

J. A. Phillips

J. A. PHILLIPS, a picture of whose store appears on the opposite page, is the youngest of Ottumwa's successful business men, a man whose capital but a few years ago amounted to but a few hundred dollars, and who today is engaged in the wholesale shoe business, is senior partner in the Boston, the big dry goods house, and sole owner of the Famous, the largest retail shoe house in Iowa. Mr. Phillips, besides being a large property owner, is at the head of a number of local enterprises and is always ready to assist any undertaking that will build up or add to the prosperity of Ottumwa. Bert, as he is generally known, is a clever ad writer, is unquestionably the best advertiser in the city, and is a firm believer in newspaper advertising. His pet hobby is the Famous, his retail shoe store which was his first venture, and which has grown under his careful management, from the smallest shop to the largest shoe house in the state. Yes, the Famous is a store of which any business man can be justly proud.

The Boston Store

THE Boston Store, commonly known as the big store, a cut of which appears on opposite page, is the largest Dry Goods house in the city, it occupies nearly 1000 feet more floor space than any other dry goods house. During the rush of holiday season this mammoth concern employs forty sales people, which is double the number employed by the next largest concern. Messrs. Phillips and Sense are members of the celebrated Scotch syndicate and occupy their own office at 47 Leopard St., New York. Nearly all the goods are purchased through the syndicate at the same prices that the large wholesale houses pay, in this way the Boston is able to save the middle man's profit. This is one of the reasons why the big store undersells all competitors. Another advantage in trading at the Boston is, they sell strictly for cash, so they do not have to add a per cent to your purchase to make up for some one elses bad debts. They are the only house in the city having a New York office with resident buyers, who are always on the lookout for new novelties and with cash on hand are on the spot to snap up any bargains that lie in sight. Mr. J. E. Sense of the firm is considered the shrewdest buyer and best judge of dry goods in the state. Another big advantage this store has is its twice-a-week shipment so that they get in new goods twice each week and are in a position to get any special suite, pattern, or in fact any article without any extra expense for express or other charges. The large increase in their business during these dull times bears ample testimony to the popularity of this house.

W. H. Cooper & Son

THE handsome residence of Mr. W. H. Cooper is illustrated on another page. Mr. Cooper is one of the leading business men and citizens of this community. He has been engaged in the furniture business in Ottumwa since 1872 and his business has kept pace with the growth of the city until his establishment is one of the leading marts for furniture, carpets, etc. Mr. Cooper is a self-made, energetic citizen, and enjoys the respect and confidence of everyone. His trade extends to all the surrounding counties, where he has a most extensive acquaintance. In public matters Mr. Cooper has always taken a lively interest. Those desiring anything in the line of furniture, carpets or window shades will be certain to secure bargains at this great store.

"The Famous" shoe store
214 E. Main, owned by
J. A. Phillips

Boston Store, dry goods
"The Big Store"
119 E. Main

Ottumwa Blank Book Company
113 E. Main Street (upstairs)

Interior of Mrs. John MacDonell's
millinery store at
208 E. Main

Corner of Main and Green Streets

Hotel Ballingall

D. FREEMAN DRAKE
Clerk Hotel Ballingall

ON the opposite page is an illustration of the Hotel Ballingall, which is the leading hostelry in Ottumwa. It is elegantly furnished and all equipments are first-class. Mr. J. C. Manchester is the proprietor and is known far and wide as one of the most successful hotel men of the west. He is ably assisted in the conduct of the house by his estimable wife and her sister, Mrs. Fraizer. The office is in charge of Clerks Edward Manchester and D. Freeman Drake. The Ballingall is one of the favorite Iowa hotels with the travelling men who appreciate first-class accommodations and cuisine. Mr. Manchester is a man of broad-gauge ideas and has always been prominently identified with every public enterprise promoted in Ottumwa for years past.

////////////

Cora B. Elgin
Vocalist and Teacher of Vocal Art
Studio in Y. M. C. A. Building, Ottumwa, Iowa

MISS CORA B. ELGIN

MISS ELGIN has had eight year's experience as a teacher, previous to which she studied under Laura Mooney McGavis, Max Kastner, Herbert H. Joy and Mrs. O. L. Fox, the latter being of the College of Music, Chicago.

Miss Elgin's terms are as follows:
Terms for private lessons in Tone Production and Dramatic expression. Higher grades—
One term, two lessons per week - $20.00
Fifth and Sixth Grades—
One term, two lessons per week - 15.00
One term, one lesson per week - 10.00
Third and Fourth Grades—
One term, two lessons per week - 12.00
First and Second Grades—
One term, two lessons per week - 10.00
First, Second and Third Grades—
One term, one lesson per week - 7.50

All terms limited to ten weeks. All private lessons thirty minutes each. Tuition payable one-half in advance, and one-half at end of five weeks.

J. O. Loch

J. O. LOCH
Pianos and Organs

MR. LOCH has been in business in Ottumwa for about nine years. He is a gentleman who is thoroughly posted in the line of business in which he is engaged, and commands a good trade which is fast increasing. His store is located at 236 East Main street. About one year ago when the Lakeside Piano and Organ Co., of which Messrs Tryber & Sweetland are proprietors, opened a branch here, Mr. Loch became their manager. There has long been a demand in Ottumwa for a first-class, high grade piano which would sell at the same price that others place cheap instruments on the market for. This demand Mr. Loch has supplied, and the fact that a ten year guarantee goes with each instrument, is positive proof of the quality of these pianos and the truth of this claim. Mr. Loch also handles a complete line of all musical instruments and the latest and most popular sheet music.

CLAUDE M. MYERS

Manufacturer of Ice Cream--Confectionery
108 E. Second Street

IN his particular line, Claude Myers occupies an enviable position among the business interests of Ottumwa, being the leading purveyor to the public of pure ice cream and delicious ices in both a wholesale and retail way. Mr. Myers located in Ottumwa fourteen years ago and began business for himself some seven years since. His beginning was humble, but by dint of hard and earnest work coupled with constant study as to the best and most modern methods of manufacturing pure and palatable ice cream and ices, he has built up a business second to none in his line in the state.

His elegantly appointed confectionery, ice cream parlors and well equipped factory occupy the building No. 108 East Second street in this city. Herewith are shown three illustrations of his up-to-date establishment. Mr. Myers personally superintends the manufacture of his cream and ices.

A very large volume of his business comes from cities within one hundred miles of Ottumwa, where he daily fills large orders. His packing facilities are of the best, and his goods are sure to prove satisfactory upon arrival. In the city all his deliveries are made promptly. Mr. Myers is one of the honored alderman of Ottumwa representing the Third Ward. He is a popular, "hale fellow well met," and deserves the success he has attained.

The three illustrations shown herewith represent as many different departments of his establishment. The first is a picture of the retail confectionery department, in which is located a handsome soda fountain. The second shows the cozy parlor, which is richly decorated and in which the ladies and gentlemen are served with the delicious cream and ices which are produced in the factory immediately in the rear of the parlor. The last illustration shows a picture of one portion of the ice cream manufactory.

S. C. Cullen & Co.
Leaders in Dry Goods

OTTUMWA has a reputation for metropolitan stores, and in no line are they quite as metropolitan as in that of retail dry goods. The firm of S. C. Cullen & Co., enjoy the distinction of conducting an establishment that is the personification of perfection in this line. This firm was founded in 1889 by Miss S. C. Cullen and H. A. Warner. The former assumed the active management, and though beginning in a small way, the first year's business amounted to over $60,000.00. In 1891 Miss Cullen bought out Mr. Warner's interests, and the increase in the business was such that an additional store room on the west was secured. The present beautiful double store is the result. With its large windows in which is constantly kept a most artistic and unique display of feminine finery. This store front presents an appearance second to none in southern Iowa. Inside, the store is complete in all modern conveniences and appointments for conducting a first-class

128-130 E. Main

establishment. Miss Cullen is considered one of the best judges and shrewdest buyers of dry goods in the state, and the wonderful success which the firm has met with, is due to her excellent judgement and business qualifications, as well as to the liberal use of printer's ink. The advertising department of the business is in the hands of Mr. T. E. Cullen, who has made a study of putting facts before the people in such an original and pointed way that their attention is fixed and their trade secured. Mr. Cullen has established a reputation for writing advertisements that are a relief and departure from the usual style.

The surprising increase in this firm's business has been a matter of much favorable comment, and it is due to the application of thorough business principles to every department of the immense establishment. By the assistance of an intelligent and harmonious corps of trained clerks who never allow their interest in the welfare of the store to lag, this firm have gained a well earned reputation with the fair sex who ever find it a pleasure to "drop into Cullens'" when "out shopping." Thus it is that the patronage of those who are looking for the latest, drifts into this well conducted store.

Thomas J. Phillips

ONE of the leading and highly respected citizens of Ottumwa, is our subject, Mr. T. J. Phillips. Tom, as he is familiarly called, is a native of South Wales, born there in 1841. He came to America at the age of eight, and settled in St. Louis. In 1868 he began farming in Montgomery county, Missouri. In '72 he was employed as pit foreman in St. Clair county, Mo. Later he was foreman of the Old North Missouri Coal Mining Co's mine in Randolph county. Still later he was with the W. B. Jackson Coal Mining Co. at Runnick, Mo. In 1880 he came to Cleveland, Lucas county, Iowa, as superintendent of the mines, and in 1889 he became general superintendent of the Whitebreast Fuel Co., which position he now holds. Mr. Phillips is a man of decided and out-spoken principles, and is strong in maintaining his views of what he believes to be right. He is president of the Ottumwa Democratic Club, and one of the liberal supporters of democracy in this section. Every one that knows Tom Phillips admires him for his honesty and high character. His handsome residence and portrait appears elsewhere.

Charles H. Philpott, M. D.

ONE of the chief characteristics of Dr. Charles H. Philpott is his happy disposition and good nature. He is a native of Iowa and was born at New London in 1860. He began the study of medicine with his father, and later attended the Iowa Wesleyan University at Mt. Pleasant. He then entered the medical department of the Iowa State University, graduating with the class of '81. He began practicing at once, and moved to Ottumwa six years ago. He enjoys a large and lucrative practice, and his reputation as a surgeon extends over many counties. He is vice president of the Wapello county Medical Society, and surgeon for the following corporations: The C., B. & Q. R'y, C., Ft. M. & D. M. R'y, the Ottumwa Electric R'y Co. and Iowa Central R'y.

David C. Brockman, M. D.

DAVID CRAWFORD BROCKMAN was born at Cedar Rapids, Iowa, Sept. 15, 1853. In 1855 his parents moved on a farm in Benton county, in which county he lived until he began practicing medicine. He worked on the farm in summer and attended school in the winter until he was seventeen years old, when he began teaching school during the winter months to earn money to attend college. He took the degree of A. B. and A. M. at Cornell college, and in 1875 began reading medicine with Dr. N. J. Jones of Blairstown, afterwards attending the medical department of the Iowa State University, where he graduated in 1878. He located at Marengo, Iowa, where he practiced until Feby. 1, 1892, when he moved to Ottumwa. At Marengo he was United States pension examiner and surgeon of the C., R. I. & P. R'y. In 1879 he married Miss Augusta Mallory of Marshalltown. In 1888 he began lecturing on the diseases of women in the medical department of the Iowa State University, continuing until he moved to this place. In 1893 he was elected president of the Tri-State Medical Society of Iowa, Illinois and Missouri. He is a member of the American Academy of Medicine, State and various District Medical Societies. His practice is mostly confined to the diseases of women and surgery. Dr. Brockman enjoys a practice which is not excelled by that of any other physician in the city.

W. R. Warren

THE present county treasurer of Wapello county is the subject of this sketch. Mr. Warren, who has the respect and confidence of every one who knows him. Mr. Warren is about fifty-three years of age and has been a resident of Ottumwa for many years. He was first elected county treasurer of this county three years ago and was re-elected in the fall of 1895. He was in the grocery business in Ottumwa for several years previous to his election as treasurer.

B. W. Van Der Veer

THIS courteous gentleman has held his responsible position for over three years and is now serving his fourth year. As the head of the local police force he has discharged his duties fearlessly and made many friends. The officers under him hold him in high regard and only a short time ago presented him with a testimonial of their respect, in the shape of a solid gold star, to which was attached a beautiful emblem of the K. of P. Order of which the chief is a prominent member. On one side of the star was engraved the words: "Presented to B. W. Van Der Veer, by the Police Force of Ottumwa, Ia., June 1, 1896." Mr. Van Der Veer is a native of New Jersey, and is in his fifty-second year. He is a man of ability and has proven himself the right man in the right place.

Otis P. Higdon

ONE of the hustling insurance men of Ottumwa is Otis P. Higdon, who is general agent for the Fidelity Mutual Life Association, and has his office in room 11, Baker Block. Mr. Higdon has been engaged in business in Ottumwa for many years' and is well and favorably known throughout the city. If you will investigate the contracts issued by the Fidelity Mutual Life Association you will be convinced that they are the cheapest and best. He is prepared to place your risks for fire, life and accident insurance in good reliable companies at any time.

James A. Campbell

JAMES A. CAMPBELL, of Ottumwa, State mine inspector, district No. 1, is the youngest man ever appointed to that position in the state of Iowa, being only 31 years of age. He was born in Warren county, Illinois, July 4, 1865, and removed to Albia, Iowa, in 1870, where his parents still reside. He came to Ottumwa in 1885, and was married in September, 1887, to Miss Blanche E. Caldwell, daughter of our esteemed citizen, Mr. Paris Caldwell. Mr. Campbell has been a coal miner since boyhood, and was appointed state mine inspector, by Governor Jackson, in April, 1894, a position which he is eminently qualified to fill. He was reappointed by Governor Drake in April, 1896. Mr. Campbell is a faithful, painstaking, careful and competent official, prompt and industrious in the performance of his official duties, and is recognized by all as a most excellent mine inspector. He is one of Ottumwa's most energetic and progressive citizens, a man of integrity, and a pleasant, companionable gentleman, deservedly popular with all who know him, and by his energy and ability has risen to a position of high responsibility.

J. D. Ferree residence
430 N. Court Street
Jerome D. Ferree was secretary
of the Ottumwa Loan
and Building Association

PACKING ESTABLISHMENT JOHN MORRELL & CO., LTD.
Ottumwa's Leading Industry.

John Morrell
& Co.
Meatpacking
Iowa Avenue

J. T. Hackworth
residence
918 N. Court Street
James T. Hackworth
was involved in
banking,
manufacturing,
and public affairs

Putnam & Bridgeman

THE illustration of this progressive firm's store shown herein will give the reader but a faint idea of the extensive establishment which they successfully conduct. Their's is the great five and ten-cent store, where bargains galore are to be found by all. They handle a complete line of Notions, Crockery, Glassware, Tinware, Queensware, School Supplies, Stationery, Books, Hardware, Toys, etc. Mr. Frank Bridgeman is the genial gentleman in charge of the business here, and the firm have built up a trade that has surpassed their utmost expectations. The house-wives of Ottumwa and vicinity are invited to examine the extensive stock at their establishment.

Left: Putnam & Bridgeman, 107 E. Main

W. S. Crips & Bro.

THE leading livery and transfer business of Ottumwa is conducted by the enterprising firm of W. S. Crips & Bro. Illustrations of their business and portraits appear in this work. Their building is one of the handsomest, best equipped and most convenient of its kind in the west. They have the largest number of Carriages, Laundaus, Phaetons, Surreys, Spring Wagons, Sleighs, Cutters, Bobs, etc. Saddle and driving horses for all ages and sexes, fast ones for men, gentle ones for ladies. Calls both day and night receive prompt attention. Telephone 134.

W. S. Crips & Bro., 219 S. Green

C. C. Church

ONE of the leading establishments of South Ottumwa is the popular shoe store of C. C. Church. Mr. Church is an active man of long experience in his chosen line of business. He carries a complete stock of high and medium grade shoes, and the fact that he is located where rent is low enables him to undersell many of his competitors, which accounts for the large trade he commands from Ottumwa proper, many people find his store a pleasant and profitable place to purchase shoes. Mr. Church is a great believer in advertising and prepares his advertisements in an intelligent and skillful manner. He is interested in the welfare of the city and can be counted on to help out on any public enterprise. Being an excellent judge of quality in boots and shoes and and an exceeding close buyer, Mr. Church has confidence in his ability to save money to all who are in need of anything in his line. He carries a full line of shoes, including the products of the very best manufacturers in this country whose goods have that high reputation which gives the public confidence in purchasing shoes which bear their stamp. Mr. Church is prepared to do the best work in repairing and at prices which are very reasonable. If you have not yet been a customer of his, you will find the utmost satisfaction in making a trial and he is confident you will depart knowing and feeling that you have secured a bargain.

628 Church Street

The Wyman-Rand Co. and the Wyman-Rand-Kerr Co.

C. A. AVEILHE
Manager Wyman-Rand Co.

THIS combination of concerns give to the people of Ottumwa and vicinity advantages which this city sadly lacked in the way of interior decorating and furnishing until these immense establishments were opened here. They began business here about five years ago and the quarters which they were then in soon became inadequate in comparison to the increase in their trade. They then had the immense store building erected which is shown herewith. Their line of carpets consist of a vast assortment of foreign and domestic makes. Their importation of curtains are not excelled by any house in the west, in fact, we know of no house west of Chicago that appeals, in high class and artistic furniture and draperies, to the lovers of good materials and solid worth than does the Wyman-Rand and the Wyman-Rand-Kerr Companies. In this building they have 46,000 square feet of sales room. The first floor in the furniture department is devoted to book-cases, also all designs and qualities in chairs, sideboards, chiffoniers and folding beds. The second floor shows a thoroughness in upholstered parlor furniture, bed room suits and lounges of the most unique designs. The third floor contains brass and iron beds, brass tables and office furniture.

121 W. Main

On the first floor of the Wyman-Rand Co's portion of the building you are completely dazed by its architectural beauty and complete fitness. This floor is devoted to the drapery stock and wood mantels. The second floor contains carpets, rugs, oil cloths and linoleums. Their third floor contains floor mattings and China and Japan office-floor coverings, such as Napier and cocoa mattings. They furnish your house thoroughly, taking each room separately and treating it in any style you like.

Messrs. Wyman and Rand concerns have stores at Ottumwa, Burlington, Keokuk and Hannibal, Mo. Mr. J. H. Wyman of Burlington is president of the corporations and is one of the pioneer carpet men in the west, and Mr. Chas. W. Rand of Burlington is interested in many large industries aside from these several enterprises. His residence at Burlington is probably the handsomest in the state.

Mr. C. H. Merrick, the well known citizen and business man, is secretary and treasurer of both concerns in Ottumwa.

Mr. C. A. Aveilhe, the manager of the Wyman-Rand Co., has been with the corporation many years, several of which were spent at Keokuk. He opened the stores here and has managed them ever since.

Mr. W. C. Kerr, the president and manager of the Wyman-Rand-Kerr Co., is one of the youngest, and at the same time, considered one of the best furniture buyers and managers in the west. About a year and a half ago he left A. H. Revell & Co., of Chicago, to take charge of this furniture house.

B. Silver, Agent

AMONG the many business houses of Ottumwa the retail clothing store conducted by Mr. B. Silver at 216 Main street, is one of the best. Mr. Silver is a wide awake and hustling business man who commands a large trade and does not miss an opportunity to secure and give the public bargains in his line that have given him success. Besides a complete line of clothing, he carries the best and cheapest furnishing goods. His ready-made suits are of that variety and grade which at the prices he sells them for, makes them the best bargains in the city. His custom tailoring department offers prices that cannot be touched by competitors. A portrait of Mr. Silver appears elsewhere herein.

T. F. Norfolk

MR. Norfolk, whose portrait appears elsewhere, is the business end of the firm of Norfolk Bros., the well known manufacturers of cigars. He is one of Ottumwa's hustling business men, and finds time to take a prominent part in the affairs of the Woodmen of the World. Last year he was president of the state organization of this order. This firm manufactures the celebrated "No. 188" cigar, which is one of the leading sellers in the market among five-cent goods. They also manufacture a number of other brands that find a large trade over this state and Northern Missouri. Their business is growing, and the merit of their goods and square methods bring them success.

O. E. STEWART
Division Supt. C., B. & Q. Railway

W. B. ARMSTRONG
Agent C., B. & Q. Railway

J. H. M'PARTLAND
Ass't Div. Supt. C., B. & Q. Railway

DR. S. L. HAUCK
Examining Physician C., B. & Q. R'y

L. W. VAN PATTEN
Tkt. Agt. C., M. & St. P., Wabash & I. C. R'ys

Calvin Manning residence
619 E. Second Street
Calvin Manning was cashier at Iowa National Bank

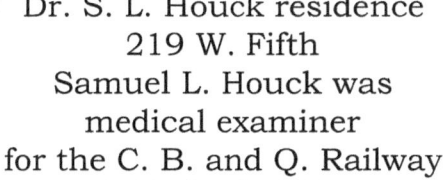

R. H. Moore residence
203 W. Fifth Street
Robert H. Moore was owner and
editor of the
Ottumwa *Daily Democrat*

Dr. S. L. Houck residence
219 W. Fifth
Samuel L. Houck was
medical examiner
for the C. B. and Q. Railway

Baker Brothers

THE above firm is composed of Messrs T. P. and S. D. Baker, who established their business of packing and shipping butter and eggs here in 1878. They have the largest and most completely arranged building for their line of business in the west. They pack and ship, annually, more butter and eggs than any house in the world, who receive their butter and eggs from the country merchants and hucksters. Both these gentlemen are progressive live business men, and Mr. S. D. Baker is the present alderman from the Second Ward. The capacity of their establishment for handling an immense volume of business is what has won their success.

W. B. Wycoff

IF you want to invest, be sure to see W. B. Wycoff, the leading real estate and loan agent of Ottumwa. He buys and trades all kinds of real estate, has money on hand to loan on first-class security only. Correspondence solicited with both buyers and sellers. References, by permission, to the First National Bank, Ottumwa National Bank and Iowa National Bank. His office is room 19, Hofmann Block.

Steck & Smith

ONE of the leading law firms of Southern Iowa is Steck & Smith. This firm is composed of A. C. Steck and Ex-Senator J. J. Smith, both gentlemen are lawyers of acknowledged ability, and their practice is wide-spread in scope. They have for years been retained in almost every case of importance in this vicinity, and no firm of attorneys handle a larger practice than do these able gentlemen. Their handsome suite of offices are located in the Hofmann Block at the corner of Market and 2nd streets.

Fisher, the Tailor

THE above title is one which the well known merchant tailor, Mr. Ira E. Fisher, advertises so extensively under. He sometimes varies this by advertising as: "Tailor, the Fisher." His establishment is located at 126 W. Main St. where he constantly carries a most complete line of every quality of suitings and pant goods. He has built up a large and profitable trade, by giving his customers the best satisfaction in both workmanship, fit and quality. His prices are most reasonable, and those wishing anything in his line will do well to call.

B. P. Ballagh

THIS successful young business man is engaged in the bakery business at the corner of McLean and West Second street. His celebrated "Entire Wheat Loaf" is sold by a number of leading grocers. Mr. Ballagh does a general baking business and is fast coming to the front in his line. He has had a thorough experience with the best and most modern bakeries in the country, and his goods are sought for by all those who have once tried them. He also conducts an ice cream and confectionery store in connection with his bakery.

Mrs. John MacDonell

IN another place will be found an illustration of the interior of Mrs. John MacDonell's handsome millinery store. This lady is located at Mrs. Briggs' old stand on East Main street, and has met with wonderful success in catering to the tastes of those ladies who are particular as to their hats and bonnets. Mrs. MacDonell makes it a point to visit the wholesale markets in selecting her stock, and as she is a shrewd buyer and keeps thoroughly posted as to styles which are or will be in vogue, she is able to secure the latest and most fashionable in everything. Besides picking up large numbers of bargains, such as sample lines, etc., which are offered to the public at reduced prices. In the millinery line Mrs. MacDonell is fast assuming the leading position in this city.

John W. Lewis

THE subject of this sketch is an Iowa boy, and was born in Lucas county in 1861. He was admitted to the bar in 1885, and after an active experience of several years in his profession in the west, he located in this city in 1891, where he has since then gathered about him a paying clientage. Mr. Lewis' chief characteristics are energy and activity. He is full of pluck and carries much ability into his profession. Of genial disposition, he has made many friends and enjoys the confidence of all who know him. He is prominent in politics and his ability as a public speaker is such that he is in demand on many occasions of a social and political nature.

Jas. A. Belmont

ABOVE will be found an illustration of the carriage and wagon works of Jas. A. Belmont, which is located at 113-115, Wapello street. This enterprising gentleman has made rapid strides in his business of late, and commands a trade that keeps him constantly busy. He does a general wagon, blacksmith and horseshoeing business, and builds to order, the best quality of anything in the line of a carriage, wagon, road-cart or other conveyance. The high quality of workmanship and material used is what has brought him success.

The Second Regiment Band
Davenport, Iowa

ONE of the crowning features of the annual encampments of the Second Regiment is the excellent Military Band which bears its name. This organization is one of the oldest, if not the oldest band, in the state. It has a widespread reputation and receives the greatest praise upon all occasion in which it participates. The officers of the band are as follows:

THEO. H. LEMBRECHT
Drum Major

Mr. Lembrecht was born at Davenport, Iowa, Nov. 16, 1867. He entered the military service as a private in Co. B., in 1893. He was appointed Drum Major in 1894.

C. F. TOENNIGES
Chief Musician

Mr. Toenniges is a native of Germany and was born there July 5, 1866. He came to America in 1886. He enlisted as principal musician in the First Regiment in 1891, and re-enlisted as principal musician in the Second Regiment in 1895. He was appointed chief musician in 1896.

A. L. PETERSEN
Business Manager 2nd Regt. Band

Mr. Petersen is a native of Germany. He first seen the light of day Sept. 4, 1865. He enlisted in 1884 and was made principal musician in 1886, and is now business manager of the organization.

C. F. TOENNIGES
Chief Musician 2nd Regiment I. N. G.

THEO. H. LEMBRECHT
Drum Major 2nd Regt. Band

Taylor & Co

THE illustration herewith shows the establishment of Taylor & Co., who occupy one of the principal business blocks of Ottumwa with their immense stock of drugs, paints, oils and wall paper. The firm of Taylor & Co., is composed of Messrs. Charles O. Taylor, W. D. Elliott and George A. Warden. These gentlemen are all sterling business men, and the firm has an established trade and reputation which has won for it the leading position in their line in Ottumwa. They buy in vast quantities and can therefore quote prices which move their goods. When purchasing drugs, paints or oils, the public can be sure of securing unadulterated and pure goods at this establishment.

101 E. Main

Iowa Water Company's Power House offices at 310 S. Wapello

McElroy's Chophouse 114 S. Market

Paris Caldwell homestead Corner Ford and Second Newton L. Arrison, the resident in 1896, was a clerk

HOMESTEAD OF PARIS CALDWELL
(The Oldest Settler in Wapello County)
Mr. N. L. Arrison now lives in this house

Wm. A. Brownell, Receiver.   Abram Wing, Superintendent.

The Iowa Water Company

ABRAM WING
Supt. Iowa Water Co.

NO city in the state the size of Ottumwa has a more expensive or better water works system. The Iowa Water Co., has invested hundreds of thousands of dollars in its plant and equipment for supplying the city with filtered water, besides the extensive water power facilities which the company owns and operates. They have laid over twenty-five miles of interminable mains. During 1895 the company invested over $25,000 in a new gravity filter plant built by the O. H. Jewell Filter Co., of Chicago, which has been proven to be the finest system of water filtering in the world. When one stops to consider how much of the human body is composed of water, and that five-eighths of our food is water, it appears to be a matter of some consequence what kind of water we use. This new filtering plant is the best improvement Ottumwa has secured in years. The system consists in filtering every gallon of water through thick beds of pulverized white quartz, crushed to fine white sand, which is manufactured for this special purpose. This holds back all the impurities of the water, making the filtered water of that purity equal to natural spring water which has passed through the cleansing of the earth. These filterers are frequently washed with the filtered water, the quartz being stirred by steam power during the washing process. The company has recently, at large expense, rebuilt the boiler house and reset and repaired their eighty-horse power boilers. This work has been done in the latest and most improved manner, no expense being spared, and we now believe the company has the best equipped boiler house in the state. Other large improvements are contemplated in the near future which will add to the already efficient system.

The Iowa Water Company is now operating under a receiver, Hon. Wm. A. Brownell of Keokuk having been appointed by the courts in August, 1895. This broad-guage business man at once appointed Mr. Abram Wing of Adrian, Mich., as superintendent. Mr. Wing being a practical and thoroughly experienced water works man, his selection as superintendent has proven to be a wise one. The putting in of the new filtering plant and other recent improvements, were done on his recommendation. In this connection it is well to state that in all the steps taken to improve the plant and quality of water, that Mr. Wing has received the hearty support and cooperation of Mr. Brownell. Another gentleman who is entitled to much credit for the successful accomplishment of the work undertaken by Mr. Wing, is Mr. Frank E. Flanders, the chief engineer of the water works.

The Ottumwa Conservatory of Music

THIS school has been in successful operation for five years, for the last two years under the direction of Prof. J. H. Rheem. There is no school in the state that has a better reputation for thorough work. At the close of the school year, June, 1895, the first teacher's certificate was granted. At the close of the year 1896, two teacher's certificates were granted. All of these graduates in this department are doing successful work in teaching. The faculty is composed of the finest musicians, and is as follows:

J. H. RHEEM, DIRECTOR

Mr. J. H. Rheem	Director
Mrs. Eva Roth	Piano and Harmony
Miss Ella Cloutman	Voice Culture
Miss Edith Spickerman	Ass't Piano Teacher
Miss Margaret Workman	Guitar
Mr. Harry Miller	Mandolin
Miss Edith True	Elocution and Physical Culture

Any person desiring a thorough course in any of these departments will do well to enquire of the director for terms, etc. The new school year opens Tuesday, Sept. 1, 1896. Location, Y. M. C. A building, corner 2nd and Washington streets, Ottumwa, Iowa.

Wm. B. Armstrong residence
441 N. Jefferson

A. W. Lee residence
109 N. College

John (illegible) residence
Southeast corner Fifth and Washington

W. H. Cooper residence
625 N. Court

CHAS. H. PHILPOTT
Physician and Surgeon

WM. B. LA FORCE
Physician and Surgeon

DAVID C. BROCKMAN
Physician and Surgeon

S. E. O'NEILL
Physician and Surgeon

C. C. M'INTIRE
Attorney

C. L. SWANSON
Merchant Tailor

T. J. PHILLIPS
General Superintendent Whitebreast Fuel Co.

B. SILVER
Clothing

JOHN W. DU BOIS
Physician

THE OTTUMWA DEMOCRAT

THE DEMOCRAT is the only morning paper published in Ottumwa, and the only Democratic daily in the Sixth District. It was established in 1852, and purchased in 1888 by the present editor and proprietor. Since Mr. Moore obtained possession of the paper it has been a success both as a newspaper and financially. Previous to Mr. Moore's ownership the paper had run down and the plant consisted of worn-out material and a broken down press. Mr. Moore having been raised in the newspaper business, was fully aware that to make a successful newspaper the plant must contain plenty of the best and most modern type and a press that would keep pace with the times. To this end constant additions of new material have been made, and in 1891 a large

H. K. WATKINS
Advertising Manager

Hamilton Kirk Watkins is listed on the title page as compiler of the Souvenir Book

Democrat offices were located in the Democrat building, 109 S. Market

ROBERT H. MOORE
Editor and Proprietor

two-revolution Potter press was purchased. The plant is now fully equipped with everything necessary to produce a first-class daily paper. The first of June last the full Associated Press report was put in, which has greatly added to the news features of the paper, and largely increased its circulation. The Daily Democrat is now the best newspaper published in this section of Iowa. The editorial and business staff of the paper is as follows: R. H. Moore, editor and proprietor; Fred H. Wilcox, city editor; H. K. Watkins, advertising manager; Harlan C. Smith, foreman of news department; P. S. Kennedy, foreman of press room; Joseph W. Hedrick, traveling representative; D. D. Smith, collector; J. S. Wohlford, advertising artist.

FRED H. WILCOX
City Editor

The Democrat Force

1. J. S. Wohlford, Advertising Artist. 2. Grant McMasters, News Department. 3. P. S. Kennedy, Foreman Press Room. 4. Harlan C. Smith, Foreman News Department. 5. C. Ed. Smith, News Department. 6. W. R. Henderson, News Department. 7. Oscar Leach, News Department.

JOHN W. LEWIS
Attorney

JO R. JAQUES
Attorney

WM. B. WYCOFF
Real Estate and Loan Broker

W. S. CRIPS

S. P. CRIPS

Livery, 'Bus and Transfer Line

T. F. NORFOLK
Cigar Mfgr.

B. P. BALLAGH
Baker and Confectioner

O. P. HIGDON
Insurance

B. W. SCOTT
Attorney

C. A. WALSH
Democratic National Committeeman for Iowa

CHAS. C. LEECH
Attorney

DR. J. N. ARMSTRONG
Dentist

DR. W. W. VANCE
Dentist

DR. F. A. LEWIS
Dentist

DR. T. J. DOUGLAS
Physician

DR. C. B. LEWIS
Dentist

A. R. M'COID
Attorney

 H. J. OSTDIEK

 W. A. M'INTIRE

 H. M. COCKERILL

 L. A. GORDON

 H. N. M'ELROY

 GEO. H. SIMMONDS

 WM. J. HICKS

 GEO. F. SILVERS

 WM. V. SILVERS

H. J. Ostdiek

THIS enterprising gentleman is engaged in the manufacture of cigars, and his store at 304 E. Main street is the leading news stand, cigar and tobacco store of the city. He has been in this business since 1891. Mr. Ostdiek is popular, and by hard work and honest methods he has built up a large and fast increasing business. He recently moved his factory into larger and more convenient quarters, occupying the entire third floor over Scott's drug store. His leading brands are the "Cuban Hand Made" and "Wapello Club," ten cent cigars, and the "Cuban Five" and "X Rays," five cent cigars.

Geo. H. Simmonds

THE printer's art is one to which many are called but few are chosen. To be a successful and artistic job printer one must love the business, and without a natural desire to become perfect in the art, no one can rise above the average. The subject of this sketch, George H. Simmonds, has but recently started in the job printing business for himself. He has purchased an entirely new and complete job printing plant, and is located at 103 South Market street, over the Democrat office, where he is prepared to do anything in the job printing line. His material being new, all work is certain to be done in the latest styles of type faces. The presswork and typographical appearance of this Souvenir are an excellent index as to what his office contains in fine job type. This Souvenir was set up entirely in his office and the press work done by him. Mr. Simmonds is ambitious to reach the highest standard of excellence known in the job printing business, and any work entrusted to his care will be given the most careful and prompt attention. He is in a position to quote the lowest prices on anything in the job printing line. He solicits a "trial trip" and will give all satisfaction, both as to workmanship and price. He makes a specialty of fine color work.

W. A. McIntire

THIS wellknown gentleman is the senior partner of the firm of W. A. McIntire & Co., the leading hardware dealers of South Ottumwa. Mr. McIntire was born and raised in Wapello county and has always taken an active interest in matters affecting the welfare of Ottumwa. He was for a number of years, superintendent of the public schools of Wapello county. Politically he is a democrat and stands high in the councils of his party in this section. The firm of W. A. McIntire & Co., enjoy the confidence of the people and their trade extends into all the surrounding counties.

W. V. Silvers & Co

THIS firm is composed of W. V. and Geo. F. Silvers who are the hustling representatives of the Jos. Schlitz Brewing Co., of Milwaukee. Their wholesale depot, bottling works and cold storage is located at 324-326 West Main street. Schlitz' celebrated Milwaukee beer has a world wide reputation and these gentlemen fill orders for a large volume of territory tributary to Ottumwa, besides the immense city trade. Their portraits will be found herein and they are both wide awake, hustling business men who have made a host of friends by the pleasant and courteous manner of conducting their business.

H. M. Cockerill

ONE of the successful business men of Ottumwa is Mr. H. M. Cockerill who conducts a popular confectionery and ice cream parlor in the Hofmann block. Mr. Cockerill is a veteran in the business and has built up an extensive trade. He manufactures his own confectionery, ice cream and ices, and is therefore in a position to guarantee the purity and high quality of all his goods. Mr. Cockerill makes a specialty of supplying ice cream for social events, parties and picnics. He is a pleasant and popular gentleman who has always taken a lively interest in matters affecting the welfare of the city.

W. J. Hicks

THE subject of this sketch has been engaged in business in Ottumwa for the past fourteen years. He conducts a wholesale barber's supply house and also manufactures a number of excellent tonsorial preparations, among which is the celebrated "Hicks' Face Cream" on which he has built up a large trade. One prominent feature of his business is the grinding of razors and clippers by practical workmen. He guarantees all grinding to be perfect and satisfactory. Another feature of his business is the sale of "Hicks' Cracker Jack Razors." These razors are of the highest standard of perfection and quality. Besides these specialties he carries a complete line of barber's supplies of all kinds. Correspondence is solicited, and all orders promptly executed.

R. N. McElroy

THIS gentleman is the proprietor of the leading chop house of the city, a picture of which appears on the opposite page. Mr. McElroy is a first-class restaurant man and a hard worker. In catering to the wants of the inner man he has succeeded to such an extent that his chop house is the daily resort of leading business and professional men who enjoy the best. One feature of his establishment is that it is never closed, and those who crave good things to eat can find it here at any hour of the day or night. Personally, Mr. McElroy is a hale fellow well-met, and ever willing to bear his share of any enterprise which will be of benefit to the city. He deserves the success he has met with.

The Ottumwa Steam Laundry

THE laundry business in Ottumwa is one which requires an everlasting push and the Ottumwa Steam Laundry has that push behind it. This business is conducted by Mr. L. A. Gordon, whose portrait appears elsewhere herein. He is a thorough and practical laundryman, having learned the business from beginning to end, and as he personally superintends every department of his extensive establishment, he is able to turn out none but the best and most satisfactory work in this line. His place of business is at 908 Church street, South Ottumwa, and his wagons cover the entire city. A big portion of his trade comes from the surrounding towns and territory. He began business here June 4, 1894, and has since secured a trade that is large in volume. Mr. Gordon is a young man of great energy and takes a lively interest in everything which bears evidence of proving a good thing for this city. His laundry is equipped throughout with the latest and most improved machinery.

JAS. A. CAMPBELL
State Mine Inspector

T. H. CORRICK
Insurance

S. R. CHEADLE

L. E. FISHER
Merchant Tailor

H. E. GREENE
Paints and Oils

MAURICE KROEGER
Piano Tuner

S. E. O'Neill, M. D.

ONE of the leading physicians of Ottumwa is our subject, Dr. S. E. O'Neill. He was born near Chambersburg, Franklin county, Pa., Sept. 29, 1836. He was reared to manhood in his native county. While employed as teacher in the district school he had access to the library of one of the physicians of Green Village, Pa., and afterward read medicine under the instruction of Dr. J. C. Richards, who was a warm friend and helped him in his professional studies. He attended lectures at Jefferson Medical College, Philadelphia, during 1863-64, after which he engaged in practicing. He received his degree at Bellevue Hospital Medical College in New York in 1872. He located at Lathrop, Mo., in 1872, and in 1876 he moved to Carrollton, Mo. In the spring of 1879 he removed to Ottumwa, and soon became one of the foremost physicians of the city. The doctor is a member of many prominent medical societies, and stands high both in his profession and socially. He has been prominently identified with the democratic party since he located here. A portrait of Dr. O'Neil and an illustration of his residence appear elsewhere herein.

C. C. McIntire

AMONG the successful and brilliant lawyers of Wapello county none stand higher than does Mr. C. C. McIntire, whose portrait appears elsewhere herein. Mr. McIntire was born at Rising Sun, Indiana, Sept. 22, 1846, and is the son of a Methodist preacher. He attended the public schools of Indiana, and later, the Depauw College at New Albany. He clerked in a dry goods store from 1860 to 1864. He graduated from Asbury University, Green Castle, Ind., in June, 1864. He commenced reading law his senior year in college. In 1859 he was admitted to the bar at Rising Sun. He commenced the practice of law at Washington, Ind., in 1869 under the firm name of Pierce & McIntire. The senior member of the firm being Judge Pierce of that city. In 1870 he hung out his shingle at Sullivan, Indiana. In 1871 he removed to Osceola, Ia., and formed a partnership with Attorney H. E. Ayres, under the firm name of Ayres & McIntire. The firm continued until 1875, when Mr. McIntire succeeded the firm and practiced under his own name until 1878, when the firm of McIntire Bros. was formed, which continued at Osceola until 1890, when Ex-Senator J. E. Jamison became a member of the firm. In 1871 this firm opened their office at Ottumwa, which has since been under the personal supervision of C. C. McIntire. This firm was for years the attorneys for the D. M. & S. R. R'y and C. B. & Q. Ry.

C. L. Swanson

ONE of the promising young business men of Ottumwa is C. L. Swanson, the merchant tailor, who bought out N. P. Swenson a few months ago. Mr. Swanson worked at his trade in the old country a number of years before coming here. He has been a resident of Ottumwa for eight years past and has a host of friends who wish him success in his venture for himself. He is a first-class tailor and will guarantee satisfaction. His shop is over the Iowa National Bank.

S. R. Cheadle

THE "Corn Exchange" is a popular resort among the business men and others who enjoy a social glass of liquid refreshment. This business is owned and conducted by Mr. S. R. Cheadle, who has always conducted his business on a high grade and commands a large trade in the best family liquors and bottled goods. An illustration of Mr. Cheadle and his place of business appear elsewhere.

John D. Stephens

JOHN D. STEPHENS, who is, perhaps, more generally known as "Jack" Stephens, is the popular and efficient chief of the Ottumwa fire department. Mr. Stephens has lived in Ottumwa over twelve years, coming here in January, 1884. For a number of years he held a responsible position with the firm of W. S. Crips & Bro., and performed his duties to the entire satisfaction of his employers. He was chief of the city fire department during the years 1889-90, and was re-elected to that position in November, 1894. His selection was a most excellent one, and was highly satisfactory to the people. He is a capable, careful and conscientious official, as well as a courteous and pleasant gentleman, and is deservedly popular with all who know him.

Jo R. Jaques

THE subject of this sketch is one of the rising young attorneys of Wapello county. He was born in Ottumwa Feb. 13, 1873. His early education was received in the public schools of the city, after which he attended the Iowa State University. He then entered Yale College and graduated with the degree of L. L. B. He was admitted to the bar in the Fall of 1894, and immediately entered as a partner in the firm of Jaques & Hunter, becoming Jaques & Jaques, through the withdrawal of Mr. Hunter. Capt. W. H. C. Jaques is the senior member of the firm. Their office is at 107 N. Court St.

Henry Copple

HENRY COPPLE is one of the solid, substantial young men of Ottumwa, whose friends are limited only by the number of his acquaintances, which includes nearly everybody in this part of the state. The greater portion of the time since 1865 he has been a resident of this city, and by his sterling honesty, courtesy and kindly ways has won the confidence and friendship of all with whom he has come in contact. He has twice been appointed to the Ottumwa police force, and each time performed his official duties in a manner that was alike creditable to himself and satisfactory to the people. During the past months he has filled the position of jailer at the Wapello county jail, and it is no exageration to say that a better man for the place could not be found. Henry Copple is a young man that it will do well to "tie to," a good citizen, a worthy gentleman and a true friend.

W. B. LaForce, M. D.

COMING, as he does, from a family of physicians, it is not very surprising that Dr. W. B. LaForce should have made such rapid strides toward the front of his profession. He is an Iowa boy born at Mt. Pleasant, in 1867. He studied medicine under his father, and in 1890 graduated with high honors from the Iowa State University. He graduated from the Chicago Medical College in 1891 and then went abroad and studied one year in Vienna. Returning, he began practicing, and also occupying the chair of Histology, Pathology and Bacteriology in the Keokuk Medical College, and is secretary of the Des Moines Valley Medical Association.

Samuel L. Hauck, M. D.

THIS good natured and agreeable medical gentleman is the medical examiner for the C., B. & Q. Ry. He is a graduate of the Philadelphia College of Pharmacy, and of the Rush Medical College of Chicago. He has been connected with the railroad for the past five years, coming to Ottumwa in the fall of 1892. By his happy disposition and courteous treatment of every one, he has won the esteem and respect of the employes and officials of the road as well as the citizens of Ottumwa. He is a member of the Wapello County, Des Moines Valley and State Medical Societies.

B. W. Scott

AMONG the prominent members of the Wapello county bar is B. W. Scott, who has been practicing his profession for over fifteen years. His specialty has been criminal law, and he has been retained in nearly every case of importance in the county during the past few years. Mr. Scott is a self-made man, having reached his standing as a successful lawyer by hard study and ability. His office is located in the Hoffmann Block, rooms 25 and 26.

A. B. McCoid

MR. McCoid is the senior member of the law firm of McCoid & Murphy who have their offices located at 111 East Main St. Mr. McCoid has been practicing his profession a little over three years, and has made rapid progress. He is a man of ability and attends to all matters placed in his hands, with promptness and dispatch. The firm do a general law business and command a clientage that is fast increasing.

C. C. Leech

THE subject of this sketch is one of the busy attorneys of Ottumwa. He studied law in the office of Ex-Lieut.-Gov. Dungan, at Chariton, Iowa, and was admitted to the bar in Sept., 1891. While Col. Dungan was busy attending to his duties as a member of the state legislature, Mr. Leech was in charge of his law business, and the following spring he entered into partnership with Col. Dungan. He continued to practice there until June, 1892, when wishing to enter a broader field, he located here. Mr. Leech has always confined himself to practicing law, and that only, and he has never handled any side issue, such as real estate or insurance. He was for years a life-long republican, but as the policies of the party have not of late years been in harmony with what he considers to be for the best interests of the people, he became a democrat, and it is likely that he will be heard from on the stump during the coming campaign.

H. E. Greene

AS a practical painter, artistic sign writer and decorator, Mr. Greene is in the lead. He has had a long experience, and by doing satisfactory work and using the best materials, has established a trade second to none. His shop is located at 110 South Court street, where he carries a complete stock of paints, oils, brushes, etc. Mr. Greene is a young man of great energy, and thoroughly understands the business in which he is engaged.

Drs. Lewis & Lewis, Dentists

THESE courteous gentlemen are located in the Tailor Block, corner of Main and Court streets. Both received their early education in the public schools of Ottumwa. Dr. F. A. Lewis, the senior member of the firm, is a graduate of the University of Pennsylvania, and began practicing here something over two years since. About a year ago he was joined by his brother, Dr. C. B. Lewis, who is a graduate of the Iowa State University. They are both young men of brilliant prospects, and are fast building up an excellent practice by the use of the most modern and scientific methods known to the dental profession. They guarantee all work, and will do the best dental work at reasonable prices.

Charles A. Walsh

IT would seem that any personal mention of this well known lawyer and politician is uncalled for, inasmuch as he is just now so prominently before the people of this country and state, having been elected national committeeman from Iowa at the late democratic convention in Chicago. Mr. Walsh is a self-made man and one of the leading members of the Wapello county bar. He has that capacity for hard work and indefatigable energy which is characteristic of the successful public men. As a leader and organizer, Mr. Walsh is in the front rank. He is honest in advocating those principles which he believes to be right and for the best interests of his fellow citizens. At a recent meeting of the national committee Mr. Walsh was elected secretary.

Armstrong & Vance, Dentists

THE evolution in dentistry during the past few years has brought about many radical changes in the methods of treating the teeth. The dental firm of Armstrong & Vance, consists of Dr. James N. Armstrong, who has been the leading dentist of Ottumwa for many years, having established himself in practice here in 1880, and W. W. Vance. The high class and quality of Dr. Armstrong's work is too well known to our readers to need any comment here. Dr. W. W. Vance recently moved here from Kearney, Neb., and formed a partnership with Dr. Armstrong. He has been practicing dentistry for the past seventeen years, and both he and Dr. Armstrong have had that ripe experience and training which places them in the front rank of their profession. Dr. Vance is one of the clinical instructors of the Omaha Dental College. He has been invited by the Dean of Iowa State University to lecture on the subject of electricity as applied to dentistry. As electricity largely enters into the methods used by this firm in relieving pain in the preparation of sensitive cavities for filling, it is well to outline it here. It consists in carrying medicines which are well known obtundants, into the tooth structure, by electric currents of suitable voltage to enter into the dental tubuli which is so dense that this is the only method that will successfully do the work without producing great pain. This treatment is called "Cataphoresis." This process has been tried for several years, is absolutely safe, and does no injury to the tooth. Dr. Vance was one of the first of the profession to adopt crown and bridge work in his practice and has used it with great success and satisfaction to his patients since he adopted it. His large experience and excellent equipment has enabled him to apply this work to the most difficult cases which have come under his care, and he has thus gained that knowledge necessary to discriminate as to the best mode to use in every case. The handsome suite of dental parlors of this firm are located in the Hoffmann Block. All work intrusted to the care of these gentlemen will receive their best endeavors. Their policy is: "Anything worth doing at all is worth doing well"—not how cheap but how good.

Dr. T. J. Douglass

THIS worthy gentleman can be truly said to be one of the fathers of Ottumwa, as he moved here from Hollidaysburg, Penn., in 1855, having begun the practice of medicine in the latter place one year previous. Dr. Douglass has, therefore, seen the growth of Ottumwa, from its infancy. He is one of the foremost physicians of the city and is respected and honored by all. The only public office which he ever allowed to be thrust upon him, was that of alderman, he having served in that capacity a great many years ago.

Burch Bros.' Koal Ko.

E. D. BURCH

THIS successful firm is composed of E. D. and I. L. Burch, who are progressive business men and command the respect of all who know them. They established their present business here in 1892, when they opened up mine No. 1, which is located one and one-half miles south of the city limits. The product of this mine proved to be the best steam coal on the market here, and they number among their customers all the leading manufacturing concerns in Ottumwa. The demand for this coal increased so fast that during the present summer they have worked the mine to its full capacity, and are taking out an average of one hundred tons of coal per day. They have recently sunk the shaft of their new mine, No. 2, which comprises 320 acres in the same locality as No. 1. This mine they are now opening up, and have built a slope 300 feet long, from which a railroad track is being laid so that they will be able to dump the product of their mine at the city limits. The output of this mine will be one of the largest in the state. When in full working order, this mine will produce 700 tons of coal per day. Mr. E. D. Burch acts as superintendent of the mines, and Mr. I. L. Burch handles the business of the firm at their office, No. 627 Church street.

627 Church Street

I. L. BURCH

BURCH BROS' MINE NO. 1

HENRY COPPLE
Turnkey County Jail

H. H. HARLAN
Adv. Mgr. Rand-McNally Railroad Guide

M. SCHWARZ
Agent Leisy Brewing Company

Grand Opera House.

337-339 E. Main S. B. PATTERSON, Lessee and Manager. **Main & Jefferson**

THE season of 1896-1897 sees this popular Theatre with a new manager in the person of S. B. Patterson. Mr. Patterson comes to Ottumwa fresh from the East with new and brilliant ideas as to theatrical management. Before the opening of the season the theater will be newly painted, decorated, drapped and carpeted and every little detail will be looked after which will make the theater attractive and comfortable. If the good people of Ottumwa will show their appreciation, manager Patterson will give them the best attractions that travel. He has allready booked over Forty nights for next season with such companies as Frohman's, A. M. Palmer's, Hoyt's, Calder's Hearnes Great "Shore Acres", Klaw & Erlanger's, Davis and Krogh's, etc. Embracing Comedy and Melo-Drama of the very highest order.

Cooperage & Poultry Co.

W. M. RIDEOUT

ONE of the principal industries of this city is that of the Cooperage & Poultry Co., under the management of Mr. W. M. Rideout, who for years has been one of the prominent business men of Ottumwa. The firm of Priebe & Smiater of Minonk, Ill., are jointly interested in this business with Mr. Rideout here. This firm conduct the same business at many different points throughout Iowa and other states. From Nov. to April this firm is kept busy shipping dressed poultry to the eastern markets and the balance of the year they ship live poultry. In addition to this they make a specialty of the dairy cooperage business, manufacturing butter tubs, firkins, apple and cider barrels. The greater part of their product in this line goes into other states. The large amount of poultry purchased by this firm makes a market for the farmer and poultry raisers for miles in every direction from Ottumwa. Mr. Rideout is a gentleman of much public spirit and always has a good word to say for his city and Wapello county. He has built up the present business from a small beginning until it ranks as the most important in this line in this section of Iowa if not in the state.

Ottumwa Blank Book Mfg. Co.

113 E. Main
(upstairs) ALF. G. COOK, Prop. CHAS. E. MOSENA, Mgr.

IN producing first class work in the bookbinding and printing line no firm in the state can excell this company. The head and front of this business is A. G. Cook, and being one of those happy mediums that is ready for either business or pleasure at any time, he has friends by the score. This company do anything in the line of book binding and manufacture all kinds blank books to order besides the best quality of job printing. An illustration of their building accompanies this. The work they turn out has won them a great reputation for correctness and quality. They make the best flat-opening blank book on earth and are willing to leave the decision as to the truth of this statement to any one who will take the trouble to compare them with other makers. A special feature of their business is county work and they are constantly at work on large orders from various counties in the state. Anyone desiring first-class work at reasonable prices will do well to secure their figures before ordering.

A. E. Woollett, Photographer

MRS. A. E. WOOLLETT

THE high reputation which Mr. Woollett enjoys as a successful photographer is largely due to his superior talent in securing the most correct pose before making a picture. His ability in this great feature of the art is demonstrated by the exquisite beauty and harmony shown in the portraits and groups on exhibition in his beautiful studio. Then the tone, finish and mounting of Woollett's photos are of the highest quality. He was the official photographer for this souvenir issue, and nearly all the illustrations herein were made from pictures taken by him. Besides the regular line of photographic work, he makes the best quality of crayon, water-color and sepia portraits. He carries in stock a large assortment of picture frames at the lowest prices for which good frames can be sold. Mr. Woollett has been engaged in the photographic art about twenty years, most of which time he was employed in the very best studios of Chicago and Minneapolis, thus receiving a valuable training and experience under men who are acknowledged to be the leaders of the art of photography. Mr. Woollett is ably assisted in the conduct of his studio by his estimable wife, who is a lady of fine artistic sense, many and varied accomplishments. His studio is located at the corner of Main and Market streets.

A. E. WOOLLETT

T. H. Corrick

MR. CORRICK is the hustling special agent of the Fidelity Fire Insurance Co., of Des Moines, with headquarters at Ottumwa. He first took hold of the fire insurance business at Milton, Ia., nearly six years ago as local agent for the Anchor Mutual of Iowa. He met with such success that he soon became special agent, and about three and a half years ago he located at Ottumwa as special agent for the same company. This gave him a broader field, and he gained a reputation in insurance circles which any man might be proud of. A short time since he received a flattering offer from the comany he now represents and he is meeting with even better success than formerly. His office is located in the Baker Block, and in connection with his special agency, the firm of T. H. Corrick & Co., conduct a local insurance and building and loan business here in Ottumwa. Mr. Corrick is a pleasant, wide awake gentleman and richly deserves the success he has attained.

John W. Du Bois, M. D.

BORN in Jefferson county, Iowa, Dr. Du Bois was raised on a farm and followed a farmer's life up to 1876, when he took up the study of medicine. In 1877 he entered Hahnemann Medical College, Chicago, where he studied three years. After graduating, he began the practice of his profession at Fairfield, afterward removing to Batavia, and later to Mystic. In 1895 he removed to Ottumwa, and is fast building up a large practice. His office is at the corner of Second and Court streets. Dr. Dubois is a gentleman who has a happy faculty of making friends of every one he meets, and is a welcome addition to the professional fraternity of Ottumwa.

Arthur L. Clark

THE gentleman whose cut accompanies this is now located at 416 Church street, South Ottumwa, where he carries and deals in second hand pianos, organs, furniture, stoves, and in fact anything in the second hand line. Mr. Clark has been engaged in the sale of pianos and organs for the past eighteen years in Ottumwa and the surrounding territory. His long experience has placed him in a position to be a competent judge of the quality and value of the various instruments now on the market in his line. He has but recently opened his new store and is fast building up a large trade. He makes a specialty of handling high grade second hand goods, and those wishing to save money and secure bargains in almost any household article will do well to call on him. Remember that pennies saved soon make dollars. Don't forget the location, 416 Church St., South Ottumwa. Parties desiring to dispose of furniture, stoves, etc., are requested to notify Mr. Clark that he may call and examine his goods.

Below left: Leisy warehouse rear 336 W. Main Street
Below right: Corn Exchange saloon 212 S. Market

The Leisy Brewing Co.

M. SCHWARZ, Agent

BELOW is an illustration of the local office and warehouse of the celebrated Leisy Brewing Company of Peoria, Illinois, the brewers of fine Rochester Beer. Mr. Schwarz conducts the business of the company for Ottumwa and vicinity, and handles large quantities of this company's product.

THE LEISY BREWING CO.

S. R. CHEADLE, PROP.

Ottumwa Blank Book Mfg. Co.

Manufacturers of the...

Best Flat-Opening Blank Book on Earth

Job Printing Done Promptly

and Books Ruled Bound to Order

Correspondence Solicited

Ottumwa, Iowa

Greene Paints!

And he's not ashamed of it. He puts it on the best houses in Ottumwa.

Signs Painted Anywhere on Anything

Paints, Oils, Brushes, Etc. Always on Hand

H. E. Greene, 110 Court Street

The Ottumwa Democrat

Daily = Sunday = Weekly

The Best Advertising Medium in Ottumwa

Only Democratic Daily in the Sixth District

Publishes the Full Telegraphic Report

of the

....Associated Press....

R. H. Moore, Editor and Proprietor

Welcome to Ottumwa 1896

The Ottumwa *Democrat* and the Encampment

In 1896 when the Souvenir Book was produced, the Ottumwa *Daily Democrat* was operated by Robert H. Moore. At the time, the newspaper was being published daily except for Mondays, under the mastheads of *The Daily Democrat*, *The Sunday Democrat*, and *The Weekly Democrat*.

From information within the Souvenir Book, there appears to have been a core staff of ten at the time, including five reporters working under City Editor Fred H. Wilcox and Editor Robert H. Moore.

The history of the newspaper is murky at best. The Souvenir Book says that Moore purchased the newspaper in 1888 and that it was established in 1852. The Library of Congress website Chronicling America lists the *Democrat*'s dates of publication as 1881 to 1903, but indicates that the newspaper had been previously published under the title *The Morning Sun*. However, the same site lists conflicting publication dates of 1894 to 1897 for *The Morning Sun*. The *Democrat* was also published as *The Democrat and Times* from 1878 to 1881.

It was later renamed *The Morning Democrat*, though that incarnation seems to have only lasted about six months in 1903, to be succeeded by *The Evening Democrat*, published from 1903 to 1904.

(Frequently-changing names were commonplace in the newspaper industry. Chronicling America lists 37 different newspapers published in Ottumwa in the 175 years the city has existed, including fifteen variations of the *Courier*, presumably all related to today's *Ottumwa Courier*.)

The *Democrat* made no secret of its political leanings, bragging that it was the only Democratic newspaper in the Sixth (Iowa) Congressional District. The first few days of the Second Regiment's encampment coincided with the national Democratic Party's convention to nominate a presidential candidate for the 1896 election. Despite the newspaper's support of the encampment, the National Guard gathering was rarely mentioned in the news sections while the convention was ongoing.

The Daily Programme of Exercises at Camp Cloutman.

The following program of daily exercises has been arranged:

- 4:55 a. m. First call for revielle.
- 5:00 a. m. Revielle.
- 5:05 a. m. Assembly, (roll call.)
- 5:15 a. m. Sick call.
- 5:40 a. m. Drill.
- 5:45 a. m. Assembly.
- 7:00 a. m. Recall.
- 7:25 a. m. Mess call (breakfast.)
- 7:30 a. m. Assembly.
- 8:15 a. m. Guard mounting.
- 8:20 a. m. Assembly.
- 8:30 a. m. Adjutant's call.
- 9:20 a. m. Drill call.
- 9:25 a. m. Assembly.
- 11:30 a. m. Recall.
- 12:25 p. m. Mess call (dinner.)
- 12:30 p. m. Assembly.
- 1:30 p. m. First Sergeant's cal.
- 3:30 p. m. Issue rations.
- 4:00 p. m. Officer's and non-commissioned school, medical officers and company litter bearers' school.
- 4:05 p. m. Assembly.
- 4:30 p. m. General fatigue.
- 5:40 p. m. Mess call (supper.)
- 5:45 p. m. Assembly.
- 6:40 p. m. First call for parade.
- 6:45 p. m, Assembly.
- 6:50 p. m. First adjutant's call.
- 6:55, second adjutants' call.
- 9:00, first call for tattoo.
- 10:00, tattoo.
- 11:00 p. m. Taps (lights out.)

Welcome to Ottumwa 1896

The *Daily Democrat* front page, Thursday, July 23, 1896

Second Regiment Iowa National Guard

The *Daily Democrat* front page, Friday, July 24, 1896

Welcome to Ottumwa 1896

The *Daily Democrat* front page, Saturday, July 25, 1896

Second Regiment Iowa National Guard

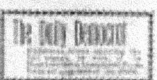

The Sunday Democrat frontpage, Sunday, July 26, 1896

The *Daily Democrat* front page, Tuesday, July 28, 1896

Second Regiment Iowa National Guard

AN IMMENSE CROWD.

More than Five Thousand People Visit the Camp Sunday.

A PRETTY PARADE

Ottumwa People Turn out En Masse to See the Soldier Boys—The Daily Program Arranged.

GOVERNOR DRAKE HERE TODAY.

A Sham Battle is Arranged to Take Place Friday.

The encampment of the Second Regiment of the I. N. G. is proving quite an attraction to Ottumwa people.

Sunday afternoon and evening fully five thousand of our citizens visited the camp. The camping ground, which is nicely and pleasantly located in South Ottumwa, is a veritable city of tents, and everything there may be said to be in "apple-pie" order.

The following program of daily exercises has been arranged:

4:55 a. m.	First call for reveille.
5:00 a. m.	Reveille.
5:05 a. m.	Assembly, (roll call.)
5:15 a. m.	Sick call.
5:40 a. m.	Drill.
5:45 a. m.	Assembly.
7:00 a. m.	Recall.
7:25 a. m.	Mess call (breakfast.)
7:30 a. m.	Assembly.
8:15 a. m.	Guard mounting.
8:20 a. m.	Assembly.
8:30 a. m.	Adjutant's call.
9:20 a. m.	Drill call.
9:25 a. m.	Assembly.
1:30 a. m.	Recall.
12:05 p. m.	Mess call (dinner.)
12:30 p. m.	Assembly.
1:20 p. m.	First Sergeant's call.
3:30 p. m.	Issue rations.
4:00 p. m.	Officer's and non-commissioned school, medical officers and company litter bearers' school.
4:05 p. m.	Assembly.
4:30 p. m.	General fatigue.
5:40 p. m.	Mess call (supper.)
5:45 p. m.	Assembly.
6:40 p. m.	First call for parade.

from the *Daily Democrat* front page of Tuesday, July 28, 1896

Since the newspaper was not published on Mondays, there was no edition for July 27.

Welcome to Ottumwa 1896

The *Daily Democrat* front page, Wednesday, July 29, 1896

Second Regiment Iowa National Guard

DAILY--22D YEAR. OTTUMWA

THIS IS GOVERNOR'S DAY

Governor Drake is Here and Will Review the Troops Today.

A GRAND RECEPTION GIVEN

Last Night to the Governor and Staff and the Regimental Officers at the Wapello Club Rooms.

A Brilliant Social Event Conducted in True Military Style.

The encampment of the Second regiment of the Iowa National Guards, now being held in this city, is progressing nicely, and everything is going along in a way that is highly gratifying both to the soldier boys and to the people of our city, thousands of whom visit the camp daily, and witness, with feelings of comingled pleasure and pride, the various exercises so well carried out by the "boys in blue"—the pride of our state, and a credit to any land; most of them with beardless faces, and many

The Second regiment, which is now in camp here, is composed of twelve

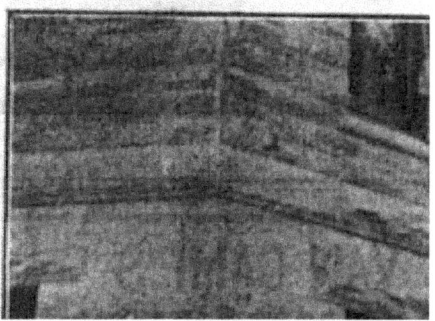

from the *Daily Democrat* front page, Wednesday, July 29, 1896

Welcome to Ottumwa 1896

The *Daily Democrat* front page, Thursday, July 30, 1896

Second Regiment Iowa National Guard

TEN THOUSAND PEOPLE

Gathered at Camp Cloutman Wednesday Afternoon.

GOV. DRAKE THERE

Accompanied by His Staff, and Reviewed the Troops—The Boys in Blue Make a Splendid Display on the Field.

THE SECOND REGIMENT BAND

A Matchless Organization Composed of Genial Gentlemen.

Ten thousand people—ten thousand men, women and children, representing the wealth and intelligence, the brawn and brain, the youth and beauty of the best city in Iowa, gathered at "Camp Cloutman," yesterday afternoon, to see the "soldier boys" as they passed in review before Hon. Francis Marion Drake, governor of Iowa and commander-in-chief of the Iowa National Guards.

The rain of Tuesday night laid the

Governor Drake left on the Milwaukee at 5:30 last evening for Cedar Rapids.

TODAY'S PROGRAM.

Today's program will be an interesting one. In the morning the exercises will be in accordance with the regular routine, as published elsewhere in this morning's DEMOCRAT, but in the afternoon the program will be varied from the regular order. The band, the non-commissioned officers and the first batallion will be inspected. There will also be field maneuvers, and firing with blank cartridges, this to take the place of the usual sham battle.

The morning exercises will consist of a drill at 5:40 a. m. and also at 9:30 a. m. At 8:30 there will be guard mounting, a very pretty exercise.

SECOND REGIMENT BAND.

One of the principal features of the camp is the Second Regiment Band—

from the *Daily Democrat* front page, Thursday, July 30, 1896

Welcome to Ottumwa 1896

The *Daily Democrat* front page, Friday, July 31, 1896

Second Regiment Iowa National Guard

Y MORNING, JULY 31, 1896.

YESTERDAY AT CAMP

The Boys in Blue Suffer from the Intense Heat.

FOUR ARE PROSTRATED

While on Dress Parade Last Evening—A Supper Served to the Members of Co. G by Their Friends.

THE ENCAMPMENT CLOSES TODAY.

And Our Soldier Visitors Will Soon Leave for their Homes.

Yesterday was a hot one all over the country, but at Camp Cloutman, where the young men who make up the 2nd Regiment were on duty, it seemed hotter than almost anywhere else. Of guns at a carry, and of course their hot uniforms being buttoned tight the test was a severe one.

It was but a few moments until four of the privates dropped in a dead faint. The ambulance had been driven on the field in expectation of such an occurrence and the stretcher was hurried out and the fallen men taken to the ambulance wagon, where they soon revived.

The boys are showing the hard work they have been put to and many will be glad when the camp breaks up Saturday morning and they once more find rest on the downey pillows they are accustomed to at home. One reason the boys have that "tired feeling" is because they work hard at the drills and wear themselves out "having fun" and keeping late hours.

CAMP NOTES.

One of the bright young ladies that visits Co. F, of Fort Madison today brought a report to the city that one of the boys of the company had died. It is said that a lady and gentleman who were friends of the "dead soldier" took flowers over to the dead "hero." It turned out that the soldier was a live man and the flowers were put to a good use in decorating the officers tent.

Every one had the highest word of

from the *Daily Democrat* front page, Friday, July 31, 1896

Welcome to Ottumwa 1896

The Daily Democrat front page, Saturday, August 1, 1896

Second Regiment Iowa National Guard

The *Sunday Democrat* front page, Sunday, August 2, 1896

Welcome to Ottumwa 1896

Ottumwa Life in 1896

From the society pages of the *Daily Democrat*

An intriguing range of ads, from the funeral director who promises "perfection in our methods of embalming" at "Telephone 5 rings -- 61" to a photographer who also sells pianos and bicycles.

Welcome to Ottumwa 1896

THE BICYCLE INDUSTRY.

Millions of Money Invested in the Wheel Business.

Diversion of Capital from Other Lines of Trade—Little Likelihood of a Collapse in the Bicycle Boom.

The enormous popularity of the wheel has made bicycle manufacturing one of the greatest industries. The figures given as to the amount of money invested in wheels and wheel plants and the persons who receive employment in various bicycle departments are truly astonishing. Of course these are merely estimates, but they are probably as near the real facts as estimates can be. These figures as given by the Chicago Tribune, which has made a thorough canvass of the bicycle business, are as follows:

Bicycle riders	4,000,000
Cost of wheels to riders	$200,000,000
Bicycle clothing by riders	$20,000,000
Bicycle manufacturers	250
Capital in factories	$60,000,000
Tire factories	5
Capital in tire factories	$8,000,000
Manufacturers of sundries	500
Capital in sundries factories	$1,000,000
Capital in retail establishments	$21,000,000
Total capital invested in cycling	$400,000,000
Employed in bicycle factories	70,000
Employed in making sundries	10,000
Employed in tire factories	3,000
Retail dealers and repair men	22,000
Output of wheels for this year	1,000,000
Output of tires for this year	3,000,000

Such enormous totals are surprising, even to those who have watched the bicycle during the last few years, and they explain the effect the bicycle has had upon certain other lines of business, including jewelry and watches, liveries, street railways, etc. The money now spent for wheels is diverted from other channels, into which it formerly flowed. The most important question is whether this influence is to be permanent or only temporary, and this involves the query whether the popularity of the bicycle is the result of a public fad, which will soon die out, or if it has come to stay. There is much difference of opinion regarding this, and one prediction is as good as another. The bicycle is certainly not a toy. It possesses much utility, and for that very reason there seems to be little likelihood of a total collapse of the boom. But on the other hand, there is good reason to believe that in time many persons who are now devoted to the wheel will seek some other and new form of amusement. It is human nature to be fickle, and especially in regard to pastimes.

The business men who are feeling the effects of the boom must exercise as much philosophy as is possible under the circumstances. It is not in the nature of things that people should stop buying watches or taking carriage drives for any great length of time

BICYCLE COSTUMES.

A Question Which Is of Special Interest to Women.

Bicycling is to be more the fashion than ever at the watering places, and at least two bicycle costumes must needs be provided for summer wear—one of serge, cheviot or covert cloth for cool days, and one of linen, Russian crash or other wiry material that looks like hair cloth, or perhaps white duck, for the hot weather. The skirts must not be too wide, for unnecessary fullness is not only annoying, as it blows back into the wheel if there is the slightest wind, but also is very ugly and ungraceful. The fullness must be quite at the back, and over the hips the skirt must fit closely. The flare must be around the bottom of the skirt only, and in the wash materials this is gained not only by the cut, but also by turning up a deep hem on the outside, and stitching it through with several rows of machine stitching. The short jackets, either with loose fronts or tight fitting like waists, opening at the neck with narrow revers, are the prettiest patterns after all. But the Eton jacket is the most useful on account of being so light that it can be carried on the handlebar if it is not desired to wear it. When the Eton jacket is used the back must be cut long enough to almost hide the belt of the skirt, and must be fitted in at the side seams so that it has a neat, trim look. The tailors prefer the double-faced cloth for their heavy costumes, as they contend that it is so much more pliable and hangs better. This cloth is always expensive and the handsome costumes made of it are rarely to be had under $50. This includes the waist or coat lined with silk. There is a great discussion as to whether light or dark cloth is better. The dark shows, of course, all dust, but somehow looks more becoming and less conspicuous, so that the choice is simply a matter of personal taste. In the linings there are some marvelous fabrics. One which looks like a covert cloth is only 15 cents a yard, makes up very well and launders well. A costume made of this material recently finished, only costs seven dollars, including all the findings. It was made by a cheap dressmaker, to be sure, who copied the model of one of the newest patterns. Bicycle skirts should never open in the back, but on either side of the front seams, and

Second Regiment Iowa National Guard

The first commercially-successful bicycle -- the first practical, two-wheeled, steerable, human-propelled machine -- was commonly called a velocipede. The inspiration for the invention is said to have been 1816 -- The Year Without a Summer -- when climate change caused by the 1815 volcanic eruption of Mt. Tambora in Indonesia led to crop failures in the northern hemisphere. The resulting starvation and death of horses made a different form of transportation an attractive option.

The machine was intially built of wood and had a rear-wheel brake, but pedals were not added until much later, perhaps even as late as 1863.

By the 1890s, the high-wheeled bicycle had given way to a safer model with same-sized wheels, rear-wheel chain drive, suspension system, and pneumatic tires, and the vehicle -- once used mainly as a toy by well-to-do and daring young men -- was on the way to becoming an everyday transport for both men and women.

Numerous dealers in Ottumwa sold various brands of bicycles. As much as ten percent of all advertising in U.S. magazines in the late 1890s was done by bicycle makers. The ad above combines the presidential race of the time -- Republican William McKinley vs. Democrat William Jennings Bryan -- with the craze for bicycles, which were often called "wheels" at the time. (The special price listed in 1896 -- $75 -- is equivalent to $2,447 today.)

A bicycling track in South Ottumwa, called the Kite Track, began hosting races in about 1890, but in 1897 a new track opened on West Second Street; it was said to be the fastest bicycle track in the world. For a time, Ottumwa became the bicycle-racing capital of the United States. Ottumwans Orlando Stevens and John Pallister were champion bicyclists; Pallister's fastest 100-mile race was completed in just under nine hours. By the beginning of the 20th century, the sport of bicycle racing had begun to wane and the bicycle track became the site of a baseball field.

Welcome to Ottumwa 1896

THE CITY.

"WE NEVER SLEEP."

Hot stuff: Gold Seal.

Smoke Fecht's Columbia.

Eat at Sweeney's Restaurant.

Smoke Peg Top—the new 5c cigar.

Havana Selects sell on their merits. Try one.

Men's Night Shirts, 75c. See them at A. D. Moss.

Ed. Dye went up to Des Moines yesterday on business.

New Pocket Books, Belts and Hand Bags at A. D. Moss'.

A free ticket with every 25 cents worth of Ostdiek cigars.

Norman and Frank Reno, of Bladensburg, was in the city yesterday.

Viavi office 22 Baker block. Health books and counsel free, 8 to 5:30.

Closing out all summer wash goods at reduced prices. A. D. Moss.

Good Shoes. Stylish Shoes. Cheap Shoes. I have them. A. D. Moss.

When you smoke Havana Selects you smoke the best 5c cigar in the city.

Daddy Toilet Soap, 20 bars for $1.00, Cheaper than dirt. A. D. Moss.

Chas Ott, of Hedrick, Iowa, was calling upon friends in the city yesterday.

Miss Emma Hande is visiting friends and relatives in Fairfield for a few weeks.

Fred C. Stevens left yesterday morning for Keosauqua to attend the bicycle races.

Walter Davis was arrested Wednesday night for using abusive and profane language.

Barn to rent, 117 N. College.

Elite Chop House for square meals.

Defies all competition—Havana Selects.

R. Kenny, of Eldon, was in Ottumwa yesterday.

Col. Shearer, of Agency, was in the city yesterday.

Smoke Ostdiek's cigars and get a diamond ring ticket free.

The members of the Presbyterian choir will meet at 7:30.

New stock of Art Linen, stamped H. S. goods. A. D. Moss.

J. W. Scott, of St. Louis, was a guest at the Laclede hotel Thursday morning.

Mrs. C. L. Walker left Thursday morning for Clear Lake to spend a few weeks.

Wm. Orr came up from Eldon yesterday to attend to business interests in the city.

Thomas Cole went up to Oskaloosa yesterday morning on pleasure and business combined.

Mrs. Zollars, the aged mother of Daniel Zollars, is lying very ill at her home on West Fifth street.

Marriage license were issued to F. A. Deveny and Martha Nash and Chas. McSparen and Miss Sophia Watts.

Ladies Umbrellas suitable for either sun or rain, warranted to wear.
A. D. Moss.

W. W. Rider, general superintendent of the telegraph lines of the Q, is expected in the city soon to give a wire test.

Best Java and Mocha. 35 cents per pound. Others ask 40c. We roast coffee every day. Wilkinson Tea & Coffee company.

Dr. D. J. Brown, the popular dentist, has moved into his elegant new home on Wilson street, just north of Court street.

Henry Mayfield, who drives the big

The Democrat's society column, interspersed with ads, the fashion of the time.

Welcome to Ottumwa 1896

Above: Men's all-wool suits, usually priced at $12, on sale for $6.49

The Hub, on Main Street, was going out of business after just a year in operation, with children's suits priced at $1, straw hats at 35 cents, men's overcoats at $2.50, socks for 3 cents a pair.

The Hofmann Office Building

All Modern Conveniences!

S. W. Corner Market and Second Sts.

Note the variation in spelling from one ad to the other.

MRS. J. H. DELANEY,
Hair Dressing
and Manicure
Parlors.

Rooms 30 and 31 Hofman Block.

OTTUMWA · · IOWA

Welcome to Ottumwa 1896

THE CITY.

"WE NEVER SLEEP."

Hot stuff: Gold Seal.

Smoke Fecht's Columbia.

Eat at Sweeney's Restaurant.

Smoke Peg Top—the new 5c cigar.

Havana Selects sell on their merits. Try one.

Men's Night Shirts, 75c. See them at A. D. Moss.

Chas. Cook was attending to business in Fairfield Wednesday.

New Pocket Books, Belts and Hand Bags at A. D. Moss'.

Hon. H. L. Waterman went up to Hiteman yesterday on business.

Viavi office 22 Baker block. Health books and counsel free, 8 to 5:30.

Closing out all summer wash goods at reduced prices. A. D. Moss.

Good Shoes. Stylish Shoes. Cheap Shoes. I have them. A. D. Moss.

When you smoke Havana Selects you smoke the best 5c cigar in the city.

Daddy Toilet Soap, 20 bars for $1.00, Cheaper than dirt. A. D. Moss.

E. F. Potter and J. W. Allbright, of Ft. Madison, came up Wednesday to see Gov. Drake.

Jasper Giltner, state oil inspector, was calming the troubled waters in Creston Wednesday.

Mrs Will Buchanan has returned home from Bonaparte, where she has been for the past week visiting.

Say! Do you want to buy Blankets now and save 25 per cent. If you do call on me. A. D. Moss.

Mis Vinnie Brown, departed Wednesday for Abbington, Illinois, where she will visit for two weeks with relatives and friends.

Miss Laura Shearer, of Bladensburg,

Barn to rent, 117 N. College.

Elite Chop House for square meals.

Defies all competition—Havana Selects.

Opera house tonight—Brady's Troubles, 10c, no higher.

Smoke Ostdiek's cigars and get a diamond ring ticket free.

A free ticket with every 25 cents worth of Ostdiek cigars.

New stock of Art Linen, stamped H. S. goods. A. D. Moss.

J. P. Lesan, of Mt. Ayr, arrived in the city last night, and is visiting his son, Harry.

Mrs. N. S. Johnson, of Bloomfield, Iowa, was in the city yesterday attending the encampment.

Miss Mary Beatty went to Ottumwa this morning for a few days visit with friends.—Fairfield Journal.

Len H. Boydston, of Montezuma, Iowa, was in the city yesterday and was a welcome caller at this office.

If the life insurance you now carry is not satisfactory, ask W. C. Linton to show you the Bankers Life.

The members of the First M. E. church choir are requested to be on hand Friday evening at 7:30 p. m.

Will Sargent, of Ottumwa, is in the city visiting his parents, Mr. and Mrs. Wm. Sargent.—Centerville Citizen.

Ladies Umbrellas suitable for either sun or rain, warranted to wear. A. D. Moss.

Miss Dora Weikert, of Fairfield, returned home Wednesday, after a pleasant visit with her friend, Miss Alice Lyons,

Best Java and Mocha. 35 cents per pound. Others ask 40c. We roast coffee every day. Wilkinson Tea & Coffee company.

Miss Lizzie Trigg is an encampment visitor in Ottumwa this week. She is the guest of her cousin, Mrs. Byran Cody.—Centerville Citizen.

Dr. J. N. Armstrong and wife are entertaining Miss Jennie Mason and Miss Lena Yeast, of Ft. Madison, during the encampment.

Society news and ads from the *Democrat*

Second Regiment Iowa National Guard

Welcome to Ottumwa 1896

SPECIAL GROCERY SALE!
NICKLIN & NIMOCKS

2 lbs wash Soda 5c	Ground Black Pepper, pure .20c	1 lb Chicago Yeast Powder .. 19c
4 lbs Sago or Tapioca 25c	Yeast Foam, Yeast Wafers,	10c size " .. 6c
Caraway Seed per lb 15c	Yeast Cream and Corina 3c	5c size " .. 2c
Pure Allspice, ground, per lb 30c	1lb can Price's Baking Pwdr 37c	Cameo Baking Powder, 1 lb. 19c
Pure Allspice, whole " 20c	8 oz can " " " 19c	Cameo Baking Pwdr, 10c size 7c
Pure ground Ginger " 22c	6 oz can " " " 14c	Bon Bon Baking Powder, 1 lb 7c
Whole Pepper, sifted " 15c	Dime size " " " 6c	

3 cans Sardines in oil	25c	All kinds of 25c Toilet Soap, per bar 18c
3 cans Sardines in mustard, large size	25c	A reduction of 10c a pound on all kinds of Tea. This gives
25 pounds good California peaches	1.00	you our 75c Tea for 65c, our 25c Tea for 15c, etc.
25 pounds good California Raisins	1.00	All package Spices put up to retail for 10c, at per package 5 cents
25 pounds good California Apricots	1.00	Tourade's Kitchen Bouquet 25c
Horse Shoe and Star Tobacco, per pound	37c	Fleis brand Extract of Beef 35c
Buttermilk Toilet Soap, 3 cakes in box, per box	7c	18 bars good washing Soap for 1.00

Three Days -- July 31st and August 1st and 2nd.   Telephone 2nd 5.

P. S. Just Received. Two Cars of Flour. One from Dakota and one from Minnesota.

Nicklin & Nimocks offered grocery goods in bulk, including 25 pounds of "good California raisins" for $1 and ground allspice by the pound for 30 cents. They also sold flour -- which they brought to Ottumwa by the train car load.

W. H. Keating & Co. bragged of the new Majestic steel range, complete with asbestos lining to prevent the loss of heat so "One can open the oven door barehanded when baking."

Baking her brain.

What housekeeper has not worked over her cookstove until her face became aflame, her head overheated and her entire bodily strength exhausted? Here comes one of the superb features of the

Majestic Steel Range

It cooks and bakes with a minimum of fuel by reason of its scientific construction. Its asbestos linings prevent the radiation of heat, keeping it inside to do the work. One can open the oven door bare handed when baking.

MAJESTIC women are cool headed women; a cool head means a healthy body.

WM. KEATING & CO. Agents, Ottumwa, Ia

Right: John Morrell & Company was the city's largest employer. The meatpacker began operations in Ottumwa in 1877. Morrells used the "Iowa's Pride" logo and slogan well into the twentieth century. Though the plant was nearly destroyed by an 1893 fire, by 1896 the facility had been rebuilt and enlarged.

Special Iowa's Pride
BREAKFAST BACON

Morrell's
Ye Olden Style
Kettle Leaf Lard.

Morrell's
Meat Market
Phone 50.

Delivered free to any part of the city.

Left: The poem on this fashion illustration from the society page of the *Daily Democrat* reads:

And now along the ocean sands
She trips, so fetching cute,
For she's cut her bicycle bloomers down
And made a bathing suit.

Welcome to Ottumwa 1896

Globe Tea Company at 216 E. Main sold many other things as well as tea, including "coffe, in package" for 20 cents and twenty pounds of sugar for $1.

People who Buy

A dollar's worth of groceries here had better have two market baskets. We don't give groceries away, oh no, but we have a way of stretching dollars that is appreciated by our customers. We sell only the finest groceries.

20 lb Granulated Sugar	$1 00
22 lb Extra "C"	1 00
Hams, town pride	10c
Breakfast Bacon	9c
Salt Pork	5c
Coffe, in package	20c

Our brands of flour we guarantee superior to any flour sold in the city.

Globe Tea Company,
216 E. Main St.   Phone 145.

Van Camp's offered to send a sample can of Pork and Beans in tomato sauce if the customer sent in six cents in stamps.

THE CITY.

"WE NEVER SLEEP."

Hot stuff: Gold Seal.

Smoke Fecht's Columbia.

Eat at Sweeney's Restaurant.

Smoke Peg Top—the new 5c cigar.

Havana Selects sell on their merits. Try one.

Men's Night Shirts, 75c. See them at A. D. Moss.

Ed. Dye went up to Des Moines yesterday on business.

New Pocket Books, Belts and Hand Bags at A. D. Moss'.

A free ticket with every 25 cents worth of Ostdiek cigars.

Viavi office 22 Baker block. Health books and counsel free, 8 to 5:30.

Closing out all summer wash goods at reduced prices. A. D. Moss.

Good Shoes. Stylish Shoes. Cheap Shoes. I have them. A. D. Moss.

When you smoke Havana Selects you smoke the best 5c cigar in the city.

Daddy Toilet Soap, 20 bars for $1.00. Cheaper than dirt. A. D. Moss.

Mrs. Dr. Roberts returned Friday on No. 3 from a pleasant visit with relatives in Chicago.

Miss Pearl Cory left Friday morning for a weeks visit in Albia with her friend Miss Grace Perry.

Ralph Brown returned to his home in Albia yesterday, after a delightful weeks visit with Ottumwa friends.

Say! Do you want to buy Blankets now and save 25 per cent. If you do call on me. A. D. Moss.

Clarence Stafford, of Mt. Pleasant.

Barn to rent, 117 N. College.

Elite Chop House for square meals.

Defies all competition—Havana Selects.

Smoke Ostdiek's cigars and get a diamond ring ticket free.

J. T. McCune was calling upon merchants in Albia and Chariton Friday.

New stock of Art Linen, stamped H. S. goods. A. D. Moss.

County Auditor Henry Wagers spent the day among old friends in Agency.

Robert Creswell was transacting business in Fairfield Friday returning on No. 9.

Mike Fraher, the hustling lineman of the C. B. & Q., was in Burlington on company business.

Ladies Umbrellas suitable for either sun or rain, warranted to wear.
A. D. Moss.

Rev. J. Pollard, of the South Side, went up to Lucas yesterday where he preached to a congregation last night.

Best Java and Mocha, 35 cents per pound. Others ask 40c. We roast coffee every day. Wilkinson Tea & Coffee company.

Charles Davis and wife were arrested Friday for keeping a disorderly house will be tried Tuesday morning before Police Judge Hall.

W. H. Warden, special agent for the Merchant's Life Insurance Co., of Burlington, was in the city yesterday and was a passenger on No. 10 for that city.

See our special sale for Friday, Saturday and Monday. We have reduced prices on many goods not quoted, 12 pounds of fine navy beans 25c, etc.
NICKLIN & NIMOCKS.

The preliminary hearing of Tom Shea has been set for Tuesday morning at 9 o'clock. Judge Hall yesterday rendered his decision in the Adams case, committing him to jail to await the action of the grand jury.

Several brands of chewing tobacco were heavily advertised in the *Democrat*, along with occasional mentions of cigars, but ads for cigarettes were almost non-existent.

Second Regiment Iowa National Guard

A ticket to the "Greatest Show on Earth" cost 25 cents and offered the viewer the chance to see high divers, acrobats, equestrian acts, parachutists, and races, along with music. One day was billed as "Old Settlers and Democratic Day," while another was "Republican and Teachers' Day."

Welcome to Ottumwa 1896

What is

Castoria is Dr. Samuel Pitcher's prescription for Infants and Children. It contains neither Opium, Morphine nor other Narcotic substance. It is a harmless substitute for Paregoric, Drops, Soothing Syrups, and Castor Oil. It is Pleasant. Its guarantee is thirty years' use by Millions of Mothers. Castoria destroys Worms and allays feverishness. Castoria prevents vomiting Sour Curd, cures Diarrhœa and Wind Colic. Castoria relieves teething troubles, cures constipation and flatulency. Castoria assimilates the food, regulates the stomach and bowels, giving healthy and natural sleep. Castoria is the Children's Panacea—the Mother's Friend.

Castoria.

"Castoria is an excellent medicine for children. Mothers have repeatedly told me of its good effect upon their children."

Dr. G. C. Osgood,
Lowell, Mass.

"Castoria is the best remedy for children of which I am acquainted. I hope the day is not far distant when mothers will consider the real interest of their children, and use Castoria instead of the various quack nostrums which are destroying their loved ones, by forcing opium, morphine, soothing syrup and other hurtful agents down their throats, thereby sending them to premature graves."

Dr. J. F. Kinchelor,
Conway, Ark.

Castoria.

"Castoria is so well adapted to children that I recommend it as superior to any prescription known to me."

H. A. Archer, M. D.,
111 So. Oxford St., Brooklyn, N. Y.

"Our physicians in the children's department have spoken highly of their experience in their outside practice with Castoria, and although we only have among our medical supplies what is known as regular products, yet we are free to confess that the merits of Castoria has won us to look with favor upon it."

United Hospital and Dispensary,
Boston, Mass.

Allen C. Smith, Pres.,

The Centaur Company, 77 Murray Street, New York City.

Patent medicines were widely advertised, with few restrictions on promises made by the manufacturers or sellers.

Gladness Comes

With a better understanding of the transient nature of the many physical ills, which vanish before proper efforts—gentle efforts—pleasant efforts—rightly directed. There is comfort in the knowledge, that so many forms of sickness are not due to any actual disease, but simply to a constipated condition of the system, which the pleasant family laxative, Syrup of Figs, promptly removes. That is why it is the only remedy with millions of families, and is everywhere esteemed so highly by all who value good health. Its beneficial effects are due to the fact, that it is the one remedy which promotes internal cleanliness without debilitating the organs on which it acts. It is therefore all important, in order to get its beneficial effects, to note when you purchase, that you have the genuine article, which is manufactured by the California Fig Syrup Co. only and sold by all reputable druggists.

If in the enjoyment of good health, and the system is regular, laxatives or other remedies are then not needed. If afflicted with any actual disease, one may be commended to the most skillful physicians, but if in need of a laxative, one should have the best, and with the well-informed everywhere, Syrup of Figs stands highest and is most largely used and gives most general satisfaction.

HOT WEATHER DYSPEPSIA.

Thousands Suffer From It at This Season of the Year.

Hot weather dyspepsia may be recognized by the following signs: Depression of spirits, heaviness and pain in the stomach after meals, loss of flesh and appetite, no desire for food, bad taste in the mouth, especially in the morning, wind in stomach and bowels, irritable disposition, nervous weakness, costiveness, headache, palpitation, heartburn. It is a mistake to treat such trouble with "tonics," "blood purifiers," "cathartics," "pills," because the whole trouble is in the stomach. It is indigestion or dyspepsia and nothing else.

All these symptoms rapidly disappear when the stomach is relieved, strengthened, and cleansed by Stuart's Dyspepsia Tablets. They should be taken after meals and a few carried in the pocket to be used whenever any pain or distress is felt in the stomach. They are prepared only for stomach troubles.

Stuart's Dyspepsia Tablets are endorsed by such physicians as Dr. Harlandson, Dr. Jennison, and Dr. Mayer, because they contain the natural digestive acid and fruit essence which when taken into the stomach cause the prompt digestion of the food before it has time to ferment and sour, which is the cause of the mischief.

Stuart's Dyspepsia Tablets are pleasant to take and unequalled for invalids, children and every person afflicted with imperfect digestion. It is safe to say they will cure any form of stomach trouble except cancer of the stomach.

Nearly all druggists sell Stuart's Dyspepsia Tablets, full sized packages at 50c. A book on stomach troubles and thousands of testionials sent free by addressing Stuart Co., Marshall, Mich.

OTTUMWA MEDICAL AND SURGICAL INSTITUTE.
THE OLDEST WEST OF THE MISSISSIPPI. ESTABLISHED 22 YEARS.

Dr. J. Jackson Crider, founder and proprietor, latterly of 41st St., N. Y., has had 30 years experience in American and foreign Hospitals. His patients come from every State and Nation on earth, and he is master of his profession. He treats all kinds of Diseases, and especially those of the "gevito urinary organs," and of the Liver, Stomach and Kidneys. Female Complaints of all kinds.

Special treatment of Nasal Catarrh; he is the only man on the face of the earth who has ever permanently cured a case of Catarrh. Board and room only $5.00 per week. Terms for treatment reasonable. You can go to Homœpathic quacks that claim to cure Catarrh, but they only clean out your nose to refill in ten days bad as ever. Dr. Crider cures it for all time to come and it never returns. Can refer to 10,000 cases cured 10 to 25 years.

DR. J. JACKSON CRIDER, Cor 2d and Washington Sts., Ottumwa, Iowa.

Welcome to Ottumwa 1896

OTTUMWA
Mineral Springs Sanitarium.
OTTUMWA, IOWA.

We wish to announce to the good people of this and other States, especially to those who are ill or afflicted with

CHRONIC DISEASES

as well as those who annually spend a few weeks or months in some watering place, that **DR. E. K. SHELTON** has the management of the

OTTUMWA MINERAL SPRINGS SANITARIUM

And will make it a home for all who may come, sick or well. All Diseases of a Chronic Nature,

Female Diseases, Cancer,
Catarrh, Diseases of Eye and Ear,
Nervous Diseases and
Surgical Removal of Tumors.

Every current of Electricity used in medicine or surgery is at command in the SANITARIUM, Massage, Etc. The Mineral Water here is absolutely a cure for Rheumatism, either chronic or acute. The house has recently been refitted, and the tables are set to suit the most fastidious. Dr. E. K. SHELTON having had years of experience in the management of SHELTON'S INFIRMARY, which was located at Bloomfield, Iowa, we feel certain that his knowledge of the care of invalids is of great value. The SANITARIUM is supplied with the latest approved appliances for treatment.

Mineral water shipped in any quantity, and to any part of the world. Write for books of information, and analysis of these waters. Correspondence solicited.

DR. E. K. SHELTON, Proprietor.

J. P. Scheying & Bro., located at 117 - 119 Main Street, offered kid gloves for $1 per pair, ladies' capes for $1 or $2, summer corsets for 25 cents each, and parasols at $2.50. "Waists" (also called shirt-waists) were tailored blouses, usually made with very full sleeves. They sold for 75 cents to $1.98, depending on the materials used.

Waste Money that Saves Money
All Our $1, 85c and 75c Waists
75 cts

For the balance of this week we'll save you one-half out of every dollar you spend here for Shirt Waists. All the waists are in the newest shaped sleeves, made well and finely laundried.

Silk Waists
$4.00, to close at .... A lot of odds and ends, sold at $3.00, $3.50 and $1.98

All 50c Summer Corsets 25c
About 20 dozen of our regular 50c Summer Corsets, made of best and one-piece netting, well boned, perfect shape, to close at 25c.

Black Figured Mohairs, 65c
About 10 styles black 45 inch figured Mohairs and Sicilians, sold at $1.00 and $1.10 yd, to close at 65c.

50c 34x45 Towels at 25c.
See Front Window
15 doz. German damask towels, knotted fringe, fancy brocade effects, with all the new tinted colored borders, extra fine quality linen—great bargain at 25c each.

Silk Mitts Sold at 58c, now 39c
10 doz. Ladies' Kid Glove finish Silk Mitts, best quality made, to close at 39c pair.

Silks
A lot of 22 inch Wash Silks. Figured Taffetas, Checks, Plaids and Novelties, sold at 50, 60 and 65c.

39c

A lot of Wash Silks, 19c

Domestics
One bale 36 inch Sheeting........3½c
One bale 21 inch Crash............2½c
20 dozen large Huck Towels......5c
Full 36 inch fine Percales..........9c
Full size crochet Quilts............39c
Best fast black Sateen.............10c

Kid Gloves
Try our patent "Close Thumb," the best glove made,

$1.00 pair

Accordeon Plaited Skirts
made of Figured Mohairs,

at $4.87

French Organdies
All our fine imported French Organdies, sold at 25 and 40c,

at 19c yard

All our 12c Scotch Ginghams, 5c

20 dozen Mens' Fancy

Laundried Shirts 50 cts
A lot of 27 inch fine

All Wool Challies
15c yd

Mens' Summer Underw'r
Our French Jersey Ribbed, with Silk elastic seams, is the best made

for 50c

20 dozen Ladies' 40 gauge, white Boot,
Black Hosiery 25c

Ladies' Capes
For the cool nights. A lot sold at $1.00 to $6.00, to close at

$1 and $2 each

A lot of $4.00 and $5.00 Parasols to close at

$2.50

Lot of 12c and 15c Wash Goods to close at

7c yd

Welcome to Ottumwa 1896

Second Regiment Iowa National Guard

BLACKHAWK

5TH VEIN COAL

Bright, clean and hard. The only 5th vein coal offered on the Ottumwa market. Unequalled as a heater or steamer.

Try one load and prove it. Telephone 6th 48.

A. C. Caughlan, Prop.

HOMER A. CAUGHLAN, City Agent

Harned advertised as the "cheapest and best" undertaker in the city

MRS. COLUMBIA CELANIA,

—DEALER IN—

FRUITS AND CONFECTIONERY

325 East Main Street.

One of the few businesses in 1896 Ottumwa to be operated by a woman.

Welcome to Ottumwa 1896

IOWA NATIONAL BANK
OTTUMWA, IOWA.
CAPITAL : : $200,000
Surplus and Undivided Profits $50,000.

EDWIN MANNING, President. WM. DAGGETT, Vice-President. CALVIN MANNING, Cashier. W. R. DAGGETT, Asst. Cashier.
DIRECTORS—Edwin Manning, J. H. Merrill, Wm. Daggett, S. H. Harper, A. P. Peterson, Samuel Mahon.

Ottumwa Savings Bank.

Capital $50,000.   Surplus $10,000.

F. VON SCHRADER, President.   FRANK M'INTIRE, Vice-President.   BENJ. P. BROWN, Cashier.
OTTO VON SCHRADER, Assistant Cashier.
DIRECTORS:—J. T. Hackworth, J. W. Garner, W. C. Wyman, A. W. Johnson, W. C. Brown, Schrader, A. G. Harrow, B. P. Brown.

The city directory of the time listed seven banks in Ottumwa in 1896. Note the amounts of capital and surplus.

FOR A FIRST-CLASS SHAVE BATHS
Go to First Nat'l Bank Barber Shop.
Corner Main and Market Streets.

BARBER SHOP   First-class work Guaranteed.
BATHS
.... Under First National Bank ....

Ads for baths, like these two for a barbershop located in the First National Bank building, were common in the newspaper and city directories.

DR. BROWNRIGG & CO.   .... CATARRH OF ALL KINDS ....
CHRONIC DISEASES.   Rupture, Piles and all Private Diseases.
Corner Green & Main Sts., OTTUMWA, IOWA.

Second Regiment Iowa National Guard

::THE::
OTTUMWA DEMOCRAT

ESTABLISHED IN 1852.

DAILY. ••• SUNDAY. ••• WEEKLY.

By ROBERT H. MOORE.

Only Democratic Daily in the City.

FIRST IN NEWS.
The Democrat has long had and still maintains this position in the city. Accuracy and Fullness in its News.

FIRST IN CIRCULATION.
The Democrat occupies this position with big odds in its favor. Our circulation books are open to the inspection of advertisers.

Office: The Democrat Building,

109 SOUTH MARKET STREET.

Welcome to Ottumwa 1896

Church schedule and announcements, published each week in the *Democrat*.

AT THE CHURCHES.

When and Where the People will Worship To-day.

UNITED BRETHREN.
East Ottumwa church, Rev. J. H Vandever pastor. Sunday school at 3 p. m., at Union Mission chapel. Sermon following Sunday school each Sabbath. All are welcome. Take Franklin Park cars to Evergreen treet

SALVATION ARMY.
125 East Second street, upstairs. Services as follows:
Sunday at 7 a. m. knee drill.
Sunday at 11 a. m. Holiness.
Sunday at 3 p m. Praise meeting.
Sunday at 8 p. m. Farewell.
Monday at 8 p. m. Soldier's meeting.
Friday at 8 p. m. Holiness.
Other nights at 8 p. m., Salvation gatherings.

GERMAN LUTHERAN
No. 728 East Second street, Rev. Geo. Laughhausserer pastor. Preaching morning and evening by pastor. Sunday school 9:30 A. M., midweek prayer and song service, Wednesday evening at 7:30.

SECOND BAPTIST.
Corner Fourth and Green streets, Rev. H. H. White pastor. Services Sunday 11 a. m., preaching Sunday 7:30 p. m., Sunday School 2:30 p. m. All are welcome.

MAIN STREET M. E. CHURCH
Corner of Main and College streets J. W. Lewis pastor residence and study 223 North Marion street. Preaching at 11 a. m. and 7:30 p. m. Class at 12 m. Sunday school at 9:30 a. m. Junior League at 3 p m. Epworth League at 6:30 p. m. Every Sunday. Mid-week prayer services Wednesday evening at 7:30. Our seats are free and all persons not attending other churches are invited to worship with us.

EAST END CHAPEL.
Corner of Iowa Avenue and Hayne streets, Rev. A. McMillan pastor. Preaching at 11 a. m., and 7:30 p. m. Midweek prayer and song service Wednesday evening at 8 p. m.

ST. PATRICK'S.
Corner of Church and Ward streets Rev. F. J. Ward pastor. First Mass at 8:30 a. m. and preaching at 10:30 a m. Vespers 7 o'clock p. m.

UNITED BRETHREN.
West Ottumwa church, Rev. H. T. Baker pastor. Preaching morning and evening by the pastor. Prayer meeting Wednesday night.

ST. MARY'S CATHOLIC.
Corner Court and Fourth streets, Very Rev. John Kreckle, pastor. First mass 8 a. m. Last mass and sermon at 10:30 a. m. Catechism 2 to 3 p. m. Vespers at 3 p. m.

EAST END PRESBYTERIAN.
Iowa avenue, Rev. A. McMillan, pastor; residence on Iowa avenue, north of Main street. Preaching every Sabbath at 11 a. m., and at 7:30 p. m. Sabbath school at 9:30 a. m.; Will Klee, superintendent. Junior Endeavor every Sabbath at 2:20 p. m; Miss Amelia Schwarm and Miss Louis Boude, superintendents. Mid-week prayer meeting every Wednesday evening at 8 p. m. Y. P. S. C. E. meeting Friday evening at 8 p. m. A general and cordial invitation is extended to all who will worship with us.

West Second street, end of street car line; S. S. Stuart, pastor. Preaching at 11 a. m. and 7:30 p. m. Sabbath school at 10 a. m. Class meeting at noon. Children's meeting at 3 p. m. Prayer meeting every Thursday night at 7:30. Sisters meeting Wednesday at 2:30. All are cordially invited. "Come and worship with us and we will do thee good."

Y. W. C. A.
The regular gospel meeting Sabbath afternoons in the grand jury room at 4 o'clock. All women invited.

CENTRAL CHURCH (UNITED BRETHREN IN CHRIST.)
Oak Ridge mission. Sunday school at 2 p. m. Preaching on the first and third Sabbath of each month at 3 o'clock p. m. General prayer and class meeting Thursday night, led by J. F. Bissell. All are welcome.

CHRISTIAN CHURCH.
No. 601 West Second street. A. F. Sanderson, pastor, residence 217 North Benton street. Sunday school at 9:45 a. m. Preaching at 11 a. m. and 7:30 p. m. Senior Endeavor, 6:45. Prayer meeting Wednesday, 7:30 p. m. Ladies' Aid Society Thursday afternoon.

CHRISTIAN TABERNACLE.
N. Jefferson St. Sunday school at 10 a. m. J. E. Woods, Supt. Preaching at 11 a m. and at 8 p. m. by Elder J. H. Bell. All are cordially invited to attend these services.

FIRST PRESBYTERIAN.
Cor. Fourth and Washington streets, Rev. Frederick W. Hissitt, Ph. D., pastor. Residence, 431 N. Jefferson st., telephone, 1st 87. To strangers: We give you a hearty welcome, and shall be glad to make your acquaintance. All seats are free. Sunday services: sunday school; 9:30 a m.; preaching service, 11 a. m., Junior C. E., 3 p. m. Y. P. S. C. E., 7 p. m., preaching service, 8 p. m., mid-week prayer meeting Wednesday, 8 p. m. A cordial invitation is extended to all to attend these services.

WEST END PRESBYTERIAN.

Sabbath school at 3 p. m., Superintendent Wm. Atkins. Gospel service Sunday evening at 7:30. Rev. A. McMillan will conduct services this afternoon at 3 o'clock.

SWEDISH LUTHERAN.

North Jefferson street. Rev. E. J. Nystrom pastor. Preaching at 10:30 a. m. and 7:30 p. m. by pastor. A hearty invitation is extended to all.

SECOND CONGREGATIONAL.

Corner Division and Davis streets. Pastor Rev. Beard. Services as follows: Sunday school at 10 a. m. Preaching at 11 a. m. and 7:30 p. m. Christian Endeavor at 7 p. m. Prayer meeting Wednesday at 7:30. A cordial invitation is extended to all to these services.

CENTRAL CHURCH (UNITED BRETHREN IN CHRIST.)

Corner Fourth and Market streets, Rev. H. D. Crawford, pastor, Sunday school at 10 a. m. followed at 11 o'clock by general services. Preaching morning and evening by the pastor. Y. P. C. U. meeting preceding the evening service.

AFRICAN M. E. CHURCH.

North Jefferson, on Sunday at 10:45 a. m. and 7:30 p. m. Sunday school at 3 p. m. Epworth League meets at 7 p. m. Prayer meeting every Wednesday evening at 7:45. P. P. Taylor, pastor. All are welcome.

THE PEOPLE'S CHURCH (UNITED BRETHREN IN CHRIST.)

Davis street, just south of Wilson, Sunday school at 9:45 a. m., James McCone superintendent. Preaching at 11 a. m. and 7:30 p. m. All are cordially invited to attend.

BEREAN MISSION.

Corner of Wapello and Johnson streets. Sunday school at 3 p. m., D. W. Jenkins, superintendent. Tuesday at 7:30 p. m. prayer and praise meeting. A cordial invitation to all.

CHRISTIAN TABERNACLE.

North Jefferson street, near the intersection of Gara street, Rev. F. Lomack, pastor; residence next door to church, No. 456. Sabbath school at 9:30 a. m. Preaching at 11 o'clock and 8 p. m. General prayer meeting Wednesday. Young People's prayer meeting Friday evening. Regular choir practice Thursday evening. Mrs. Carrie Smith organist. Teacher's meeting Tuesday evening. Ladies sewing circles Thursday afternoon. All are cordially invited to attend these services.

FIRST BAPTIST.

Preaching, Sunday, June 21, at 10:45 a. m. and 8 p. m. by Rev. Howard Tilden of Cedar Rapids. Sunday School 9:30 a. m. Everybody invited to these services.

There will be no services at the First Baptist church today, except the regular Sunday school. Rev. Henry Tilden of Boston, Mass., will supply the pulpit made vacant by Rev. Henry Williams, for several months. He will begin next Sunday, the 28th. Rev. Tilden is a Baptist minister of much ability, lately from Boston, though for some time he has not occupied a pulpit. He has not been called to Ottumwa, but is simply to preach temporarily.

FIRST M. E.

At the First M. E. church today preaching at 11 a. m. and 8 p. m. Subject this morning "Christian Citizenship," and this evening's topic, "Our Advocate."

TRINITY EPISCOPAL CHURCH

Rev. J. Hollister Lynch, Rector, Sixth Sunday after Trinity July 12th, 1896. Sunday school at 9:45 a. m. Holy communion 7:45 a. m. Morning prayer and sermon 11 a. m. Evening prayer and sermon, 8 p. m.

Because of the extreme heat there will be no services at Trinity church on Sunday evenings, until September 6th. The Sunday school and morning services will be as usual.

FIRST CONGREGATIONAL.

The pastor, Rev. L. F. Berry, will conduct the usual services. Theme in the morning, "Our Lord's Estimate of Man's Worth." In the evening a service of Song. All are requested to bring "Crowning Glory." Sunday School at 9:45 a. m., E. Adams Holt, Superintendent. C. E. meetings at 3 p. m., and 7 p. m. A hearty welcome is extended to all. Good music. Seats free.

"Have you no pen and ink?" said a doctor to a poor woman, whose boy he was attending.

"No."

"Well, I have lost my pencil; give me a bit of chalk."

The doctor chalked a prescription on the door, telling her to give it to her son when he awoke.

"Take it my boy, take it," said the old woman, lifting the door from its hinges and carrying it to the poor boy when he opened his eyes. "I don't know how you are to do it, but the doctor says it is good, and you had better try to bolt it."—Spare Moments.

Welcome to Ottumwa 1896

The railroad timetable published daily in the Ottumwa *Democrat* lists nearly 30 passenger trains serving Ottumwa each day, as well as "fast mail trains" and freights. Three depots served six separate railroads listed here as passing through the city. The Chicago, Burlington & Quincy (forerunner of today's Burlington Northern) and the Chicago, Rock Island & Pacific both used Union Depot. Iowa Central, the Wabash, and the Chicago, Milwaukee & St. Paul used the Jefferson Street Union Station (often called the Wabash depot). The Chicago, Ft. Madison & Des Moines used a depot located at the foot of Union Street. A seventh railroad mentioned here did not operate in Ottumwa but offered connections for passengers once they reached Burlington. Other depots in the city also handled passenger and freight traffic.

Union Depot as it would have looked about the time of the Encampment. The depot was remodeled in 1950; the tower and peaked roof were removed and the building was extended and refaced with stone. The water in foreground is the race, a secondary water channel diverted from the Des Moines River. The race was later filled in and the main river channel relocated when the river was straightened in the late 1950s.

(8)

TO THE TRAVELING PUBLIC.

The Burlington Route

Offers unsurpassed facilities in the way of

COMFORT, SPEED AND SAFETY.

Solid Vestibule Trains

BETWEEN LAKE MICHIGAN AND THE ROCKY MOUNTAINS. BAGGAGE CHECKED THROUGH TO DESTINATION,

AND ALL CONNECTIONS IN UNION DEPOTS.

THE BEST ROUTE TO

All Colorado Resorts,

The Hot Springs of South Dakota,

And all Pacific Coast Points.

P. S. EUSTIS,

G. P. & T. Agt.,

Chicago.

Welcome to Ottumwa 1896

THE CITY.

"WE NEVER SLEEP."

Hot stuff: Gold Seal.

Smoke Fecht's Columbia.

Eat at Sweeney's Restaurant.

Smoke Peg Top—the new 5c cigar.

Havana Selects sell on their merits. Try one.

Men's Night Shirts, 75c. See them at A. D. Moss.

D. J. Thayer, of Chariton, was a Sunday visitor in Ottumwa.

New Pocket Books, Belts and Hand Bags at A. D. Moss'.

Miss Ollie Schreiner, of Albia, is a guest of Ottumwa friends.

Viavi office 22 Baker block. Health books and counsel free, 8 to 5:30.

Closing out all summer wash goods at reduced prices. A. D. MOSS.

Good Shoes. Stylish Shoes. Cheap Shoes. I have them. A. D. MOSS.

When you smoke Havana Selects you smoke the best 5c cigar in the city.

Daddy Toilet Soap, 20 bars for $1.00. Cheaper than dirt. A. D. MOSS.

O. Waddell, of Oskaloosa, will visit among Ottumwa friends during the encampment.

Miss Phoebe Thurston left on No. 9 Monday for Thayer, Iowa, to visit for a couple of weeks at home.

Say! Do you want to buy Blankets now and save 25 per cent. If you do call on me. A. D. MOSS.

Miss Marie Pennington, of Bloomfield, spent Sunday among Ottumwa friends, on her return from a visit at Albia.

A safe, simple and effective remedy for indigestion is a dose of Ayer's Pills. Try the Pills and make your meals enjoyable.

Miss Abbie Cooper returned Monday morning from Pella and Des Moines, where she has been visiting relatives and friends for the past week.

Have just received another invoice of Muslin Underwear. For style, quality and price it can't be beaten.
A. D. MOSS.

Barn to rent, 117 N. College.

Elite Chop House for square meals.

Defies all competition—Havana Selects.

Smoke Ostdiek's cigars and get a diamond ring ticket free.

Ted Cooper is enjoying a brief visit with Oskaloosa friends.

A free ticket with every 25 cents worth of Ostdiek cigars.

Squire Moore, of Eddyville, was in Ottumwa yesterday on business.

New stock of Art Linen, stamped H. S. goods. A. D. MOSS.

Walter Abegg, of Blakesburg, was an over Sunday visitor in the metropolis.

Thos. Hinks was a Rock Island passenger yesterday morning for Laddsdale.

Miss Lillian Thode, of Blakesburg, Iowa, spent Sunday among Ottumwa friends.

Miss Florence Cram left last evening for Hiteman, where she will spend a few days with friends.

If the life insurance you now carry is not satisfactory, ask W. C. Linton to show you the Bankers Life.

Henry Wright, of Centerville, visited among the members of Company E at Camp Cloutman Sunday.

B. T. Raines, a prominent hardware merchant of Fairfield, was greeting his many Ottumwa friends Monday.

Ladies Umbrellas suitable for either sun or rain, warranted to wear.
A. D. MOSS.

Best Java and Mocha, 35 cents per pound. Others ask 40c. We roast coffee every day. Wilkinson Tea & Coffee company.

Oskaloosa Herald: Miss Mabel Hooyer, who has been visiting her sister, Mrs. Courtney, returned to her home in Ottumwa this morning.

Miss Nora Elder, who is attending Normal in the city returned yesterday from Highland Center, where she spent Sunday with her parents.

There were two drunks before his honor Monday morning. They were fined $10 and costs one paid and the other will study geology for three days.

Mr. and Mrs. Henry Martin and children returned Monday evening from Centerville, where they went to attend the funeral of Mrs. Martin's father, Wm. Addice.

Ostdiek cigars are the best.

Capt. J. G. Hutchinson was in Mystic Monday on business.

E. S. Fist was transacting business in Mt. Pleasant Monday.

Mrs. S. A. Miller, of Eldon, was a guest of Ottumwa friends Monday.

Thos. Johnson, of Mt. Pleasant, spent Sunday with friends in Ottumwa.

Corsets. A fine stock and prices the lowest. A. D. MOSS.

S. W. Epman, of Des Moines, was a business visitor in the city yesterday.

Howard Shearer, of Agency, was a business visitor in Ottumwa yesterday.

Jim Van Emmons was a passenger south on the Milwaukee for a few days business trip.

Miss Eva Crider left Monday morning for a brief visit with relatives and friends in Fairfield.

Miss Lenora Sprague, of South Ottumwa, has returned from a brief visit with Eddyville friends.

Mrs. Lizzie Kimmel and little daughter, Fay, returned Monday evening from a week's visit at Eldon.

Miss Bertha Wolcott, of Keokuk, will arrive here Wednesday, and will be the guest of Miss Lorene Finley.

Carpets, Rugs, Oil Cloths and Matting. The low prices still prevail.
A. D. MOSS.

Dr. C. H. Philpott and wife returned Monday morning from Clear Lake, where they have been enjoying a week's outing.

Miss Kate Detrich, of South Ottumwa was adjudged insane yesterday and was taken to the asylum at Mt. Pleasant by Sheriff Stodghill.

The case of the state against Tom Healy was continued by agreement until next Thursday morning at 9 o'clock in Justice Pollard's court.

Dr. W. B. La Force has returned from a week's trip trip to Clear Lake. While there the doctor attended a State Medical meeting held there.

Miss Lillian Sutton, daughter of ex-Marshal Sutton, of Fairfield, arrived in the city Monday evening and will visit relatives and friends during the encampment.

Some sneak thief stole a 20 foot canvass stock cover from Andrew Swanson on the South Side Sunday night. Andy has blood in his eye and it will not be well for the thief should he catch him.

Society news and ads from the *Democrat*

Second Regiment Iowa National Guard

PHILLIPS & RUPE,
314 CHURCH ST., SOUTH OTTUMWA.

FLOUR, HAY AND FEED
OF ALL KINDS.

Orders for Agricultural Machinery of all makes promptly filled.

The St. Louis department store, also known as W. J. Donelan & Co., sold "wash goods" and "dress goods" for home seamstresses, including wool fabrics priced from seven and a half cents a yard all the way up to 35 cents a yard.

Welcome to Ottumwa 1896

THE CITY.

"WE NEVER SLEEP."

Hot stuff: Gold Seal.

Smoke Fecht's Columbia.

Eat at Sweeney's Restaurant.

Smoke Peg Top—the new 5c cigar.

Havana Selects sell on their merits. Try one.

Men's Night Shirts, 75c. See them at A. D. Moss.

O. D. Tisdale was in Chillicothe Tuesday on business.

New Pocket Books, Belts and Hand Bags at A. D. Moss'.

Viavi office 22 Baker block. Health books and counsel free, 8 to 5:30.

Closing out all summer wash goods at reduced prices. A. D. Moss.

Good Shoes. Stylish Shoes. Cheap Shoes. I have them. A. D. Moss.

When you smoke Havana Selects you smoke the best 5c cigar in the city.

Daddy Toilet Soap, 20 bars for $1.00. Cheaper than dirt. A. D. Moss.

Mrs. J. H. Lloyd and son Basil, of Cedar Rapids are visiting at the home of A. P. Peterson.

Mrs. Dena Young, of Ottumwa, visited Mr. and Mrs. J. C. Morrison, on Saturday.—Albia Union.

W. H. Farmer will leave this morning for Indianola, Iowa, on a two weeks pleasure and business trip.

The wheelmen of Chariton will be "at home" to clubs from neighboring towns on Sunday, August 2nd.

Private Harry Taylor, of Keokuk, came up yesterday morning and joined his company at Camp Cloutman.

Say! Do you want to buy Blankets now and save 25 per cent. If you do call on me. A. D. Moss.

Miss Kate Kelly terminated a weeks visit in Albia on Saturday and returned to her home in Ottumwa.—Albia

Barn to rent, 117 N. College.

Elite Chop House for square meals.

Defies all competition—Havana Selects.

Smoke Ostdick's cigars and get a diamond ring ticket free.

Miss Lulu Brunt, of Sigourney, is visiting Ottumwa friends.

A free ticket with every 25 cents worth of Ostdick cigars.

L. C. Phillips and daughter, of Fairfield, were Ottumwa visitors Tuesday.

New stock of Art Linen, stamped H. S. goods. A. D. Moss.

Mrs. J. Ferris has gone to Denver, Colorado, to spend the remainder of the summer.

J. P. Lesan, of Mt. Ayr, arrived in the city last night, and is visiting his son, Harry.

If the life insurance you now carry is not satisfactory, ask W. C. Linton to show you the Bankers Life.

Sant Kirkpatrick will address an open air meeting on the South Side on Monday evening, August 3d.

C. C. Doty and family have returned from Minnesota, where they have been enjoying a three week's visit.

Ladies Umbrellas suitable for either sun or rain, warranted to wear.
A. D. Moss.

Miss Mable Howard, of Sigourney, returned Tuesday evening from a visit at Red Oak, and is a guest of Ottumwa friends.

Engineer Ed. Gavny, of the Chariton branch, returned home yesterday morning, after a brief visit with Ottumwa friends.

Best Java and Mocha, 35 cents per pound. Others ask 40c. We roast coffee every day. Wilkinson Tea & Coffee company.

Reduced to 10 cents to all parts of the Grand opera house, to see the Reeves Comedy Co. tonight and balance of week.

George Elliott, city editor of the Courier, has returned from Eddyville, where he spent a week, visiting friends and enjoying a needed rest.

A young man by the name of Cicero

Society news and ads from the *Democrat*

A selection from the Revised Ordinances of the City of Ottumwa, Iowa of 1898

Health and Safety

391. Sec. 6. Quarantine shall be established and maintained in each and every case for the period named herein, to-wit:
    Scarlet Fever (scarletina, scarlet rash), thirty-five days.
    Diphtheria (membraneous croup), thirty-five days.
    Small Pox -- Forty days.
    Asiatic Cholera -- Twenty-one days.

396. Sec. 11. No person shall give, lend or sell, or offer for sale any clothing or other articles liable to convey infection of any contagious disease unless the same have been disinfected and such disinfection approved by the mayor.

402. Sec. 17. Every person, firm, or corporation, or agent, or employe [sic] thereof, who shall sell milk or cream from a wagon, depot or store; or sell or deliver milk or cream to a hotel, restaurant, boarding house, public place or private residence in this city shall furnish satisfactory evidence that said milk or cream is taken from cows that are free from tuberculosis.

405. Sec. 20. A body dead from small pox must be immediately wrapped in a cloth saturated with the strongest disinfectant solution, without previous washing, and buried deep, and no body dead from this disease shall under any circumstances, or any lapse of time be disinterred.

406. Sec. 21. The body of a person who has died from Asiatic cholera, yellow fever, leprosy, diphtheria (membraneous croup), scarlet fever, (scarletina or scarlet rash), must not be removed from the sick room until it has been wrapped in a cloth saturated with a solution of corrosive sublimate (one ounce to six gallons of water), and then tightly enclosed in a coffin. The body shall then be buried immediately without the attendance of any person other than is necessary for the interment thereof.

Midwife

Nyquist Mrs O, 527 e Main

Magnetic Healers

Nichols J W, 811 w Second

Listing of medical specialties in city directory of 1894-95

407. Sec. 22. No public funeral shall be held of [sic] any person who has died from either of said diseases named in sections twenty and twenty-one, and no public funeral shall be held in a house, nor on any premises where there is a case of, nor where a death has recently occurred from either of said diseases.

437. Sec. 1. Privy vaults must be constructed hereafter as follows: Each building situated on an unsewered street or alley must have a privy vault not less than three (3) feet wide and four (4) feet deep, lined with hard brick, laid in cement mortar, cemented on the inside with Portland cement, proved to be water tight.

438. Sec. 2. Privy vaults shall not be located within two (2) feet of party lines or within twenty (20) feet from any dwelling house or tenant house, or within fifty (50) feet of a well.

> 134. Sec. 5. The chief of the fire department shall be superintendent of the fire alarm telegraph and all the wires, apparatus, signal stations and keys thereto, and keep the same in complete repair as far as practicable. The work in repairing the same shall be done by the members of the fire department. He shall distribute the keys to signal stations, keep a record of such distribution and take receipts for keys when given out.

Welcome to Ottumwa 1896

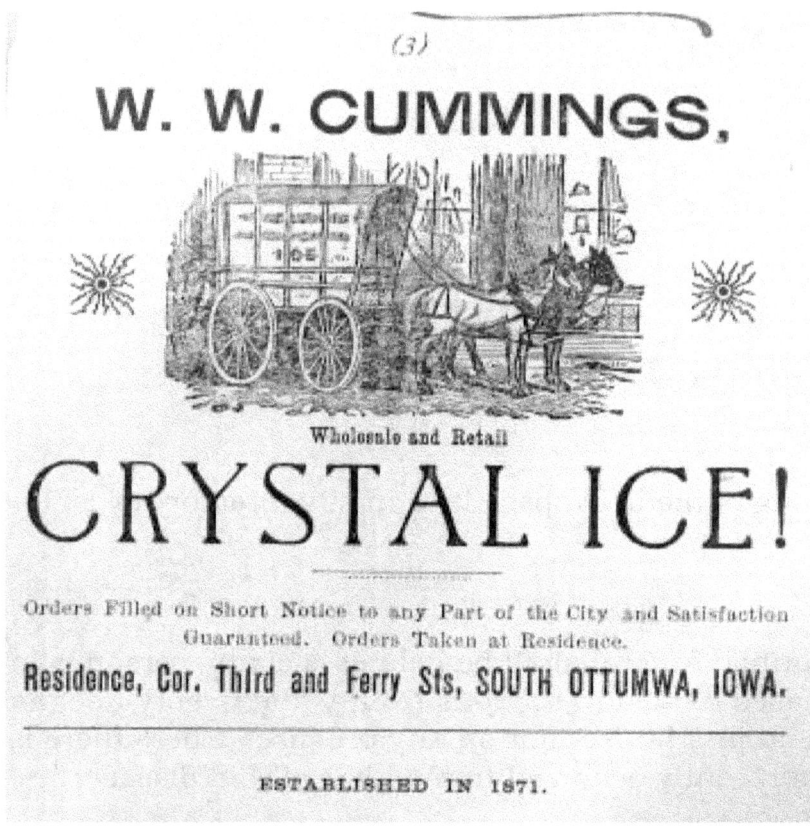

440. Sec. 1. It shall be unlawful for any person, partnership or corporation to cut, store, and preserve for domestic purposes any ice from what is known as Harrow's branch, or the race below the guard locks, or from the Des Moines river at any point below Milner street, if extended across said river. (Except by special permit from the board of health.)

441. Sec. 2. It shall be unlawful to use any horse upon the ice whose feet have not been thoroughly cleansed before going upon the same, and all droppings from horses shall be immediately removed.

441. Sec. 3. Ice for domestic purposes shall not be floated down the race below the drain entering the race at or near Curran & Rogers' ice house, or floated down the river below the point above designated in this ordinance, or in any manner contaminated.

443. Sec. 4. Any person, partnership or corporation taking ice from any of the prohibited districts herein mentioned, or from any other impure source for sale for domestic purposes, or selling the same for domestic purposes, taken from the prohibited districts, or impure source, shall, upon conviction thereof be fined in any sum not less than ten dollars nor more than fifty dollars for each and every offense, and shall stand committed to jail until said fine and costs are paid.

Second & Washington

Ottumwa Commercial College.

Located in the New
Y. M. C. A. BUILDING.

Thoroughly Equipped with all Modern Improvements.

Bookkeeping, both Single and Double Entry, Commercial Law, Commercial Arithmetic, Actual Business, Penmanship, etc. Complete Shorthand Department—leading system taught. Leading Typewriting Machines in use.

SEND FOR CATALOGUE.

Rooms of the Young Men's Christian Association—Open every day except Sunday from 9 a. m. until 10 p. m. Visitors Welcome.

Welcome to Ottumwa 1896

Four streetcars meeting at Second and Market. Electric-powered streetcars started service in Ottumwa in 1889. One of the cars shown here serves South Ottumwa, while another serves the east end, including the area of Franklin Park. The building at center, under the street light which hangs above the intersection, is J.W. Edgerly, now the site of US Bank.

Streetcars

Be it ordained by the City Council of the City of Ottumwa:

218. Section 1. That authority for thirty years is hereby granted to said Ottumwa Electric Railway, its successors and assigns, to locate, construct and operate a street railway, having a four foot eight and one-half inch standard guage [sic], by electric or other motor power, other than steam power, upon the following streets, bridges and public grounds of and in the city of Ottumwa, that is to say:

On and along Market street from Main street over and across the Des Moines river bridge, located over the Des Moines river at the foot of Market street, together with all approaches or fills leading to and upon said bridge....

207. Section 9. 1. No car shall be run at a greater average rate of speed, including stoppages to take on and leave off passengers, than eight miles an hour in the business part of the city, and twelve miles an hour in the residence portion thereof, nor less than an average of five miles an hour in the business portion of the city, and eight miles an hour in the residence portion thereof; except at those times and

places where such rate of speed would be carelessness or negligence. While cars are turning corners from one street to another they shall not be moved to exceed five miles an hour.

6. All proper care shall be used by conductors and drivers to prevent injury to teams, carriages, wagons, and other vehicles, as well as to all persons.

7. Conductors shall use proper diligence to prevent ladies and children from entering and leaving the cars while said cars are in motion.

8. Conductors shall announce to passengers, in a distinct tone, the names of all streets crossed, as the cars approach said cross streets, and they shall observe the same rule when nearing any depot or hotel on its line.

224. Sec. 7. The rate of fare upon any route or line of said street railway shall not exceed five cents for any passenger, one trip, one way, over the entire line covered by this franchise, and on the same continuous trip, also to include over any other line of street railway owned or operated by said company within said city to the end of such one trip one way.

225. Sec. 8. The cars of said street railway shall be entitled to the track in all cases. When a team or vehicle shall be met or overtaken upon any of the street railways of said company, such team or vehicle shall give way to such car.

Bicycles

40. Sec. 3. It shall be unlawful for any person to ride with bicycle along any of the public business streets of the city of Ottumwa, at a greater rate of speed than eight miles an hour, or across the crossings in said portion of the city at a higher rate of speed than five (5) miles per hour, except on special occasions when the permssion of the mayor of the city of Ottumwa, Iowa, has been granted, as hereinafter provided.

41. Sec. 4. The mayor of the city in his discretion may grant permission free of charge to any bicycle club or bicycle organization to give exhibits of their speed upon any of the public streets of the city between certain hours specified in his permit.

No speed limits for motor vehicles (other than streetcars) were included in the 1898 city ordinances.

Welcome to Ottumwa 1896

As the presidential campaign neared election day, the Democratic nominee, William Jennings Bryan -- who had campaigned across the country by train, while William McKinley held rallies in his own town (many on his front porch) -- spent a day in Ottumwa.

BRYAN'S DAY.

Official Program for Bryan's Day at Ottumwa, Saturday, Oct. 31.

Following is the official program for Bryan's day at Ottumwa, Oct. 31, '96:

W. H. C. Jaques, chief marshal.

Reception committee and marching clubs will meet at democratic headquarters at 7:30 a. m. Everybody invited to come.

March from headquarters, headed by Schwabkey's band and platoon of police to opera house, unite there with the Bloomfield club. From there march to Evergreen street crossing of the C. B. & Q. track, (near packing house), where W. J. Bryan will make a ten minute speech. Mr. Bryan will then pass through the open ranks of the parade and be escorted up town on Main street to the Grand opera house, and make a short speech. From the Grand opera house he will be escorted to the park where he will again speak, after which he will be escorted to Union depot. The reception committee and marching clubs will preserve ranks until they reach the depot.

Horse parade—The horses will rendezvous at and near the park at 12:30 p. m. Parade to start at 1 p. m. The line will form on Fourth street, head of column at Wapello in the following order:

Platoon of police.

Chief marshal and aids.

Sixteen girls in white and one in yellow.

Riding clubs and bands as assigned by the aids.

Route of march—South on Wapello to Second, west on Second to McLean, south on McLean to Main, east on Main to Union, north on Union to Second, west on Second to Court, north on Court to Park, where the parade will disband as it arrives.

Marshal—Capt. W. C. Jaques.

Assistant marshals—L. C. Hendershott, Capt. W. H. Kitterman, Seneca Cornell, Milo Reno, Capt. S. B. Evans, Judge A. C. Steck, J. H. Fugate, J. N. Baker, B. E Guegerty, Chas. Ayers, L. O. Johnson, B. W. Scott, D. C. Chisman, Dr. L. Torrence, Lafe Dudgeon, D. V. Drake, Gideon Dotts, Jr., Chas. Parker, U. G. Hawthorne, C. C. Leech, John Mader, David Sauterne.

James Gray will have charge of the arrangements at the Grand this morning, and with the assistance of a competent corps of ushers, will see that all are comfortably seated as long as the seats hold out.

AT THE PACKING HOUSE.

Wm. J. Bryan will speak at the packing house at 8:15 this morning.

Second Regiment Iowa National Guard

From the front page of the *Daily Democrat*, Saturday, October 31, 1896

The *Daily Democrat* front page, Wednesday, November 4, 1896, announcing the election of William McKinley

Second Regiment Iowa National Guard

SOUND MONEY AND PROSPERITY

McKinley and Hobart Elected by an Overwhelming Majority. Bryan Badly Beaten.

Free Silver and Repudiation Knocked Higher than Gilroy's Kite--Too Dead to Skin.

"AND THE BLOW ALMOST KILLED"---WILLIE.

McKinley Makes a Home Run. Bryan Didn't Reach First Base. Palmer Makes a Sacrifice Hit.

The election in this city Tuesday passed off quietly, and the vote polled was an unusually large one, probably the largest ever known in the history of the city. As soon as the polls opened in the morning the voting began in earnest, and the ballots were deposited as rapidly as they could be taken care of by the judges and clerks.

From the *Daily Democrat* front page on Wednesday, November 4, 1896, the day after the election

Welcome to Ottumwa 1896

The World in 1896

In 1896, the President of the United States was Grover Cleveland, the Vice President was Adlai E. Stevenson (his son Adlai E. Stevenson II ran for President in 1952 and 1956 against Dwight D. Eisenhower). The nation was ramping up for the 1896 election pitting William McKinley against William Jennings Bryan. At the Democratic convention, Bryan delivered what would become known as his "Cross of Gold" speech, calling for the nation's monetary standard to be based on silver as well as gold in order to ease economic development. He had not been seen as a viable candidate until his speech took the convention by storm. Bryan campaigned across the entire country by train, including a stop in Ottumwa just days before the election.

Utah was admitted to the Union as the 45th state and gold was discovered in Alaska's Klondike.

In the case of *Plessy v. Ferguson,* the U.S. Supreme Court introduced the concept of "separate but equal" to uphold the doctrine of racial segregation.

Films of the year included *Rip's Twenty Years' Sleep, McKinley at Home* (a silent film re-enactment of his nomination for President by the Republican party), *The Kiss* starring May Irwin, and a short, silent-film documentary called *Dancing Darkies*.

The Dow Jones Industrial Average was first calculated by Charles Dow in May 1896, based on twelve industrial stocks; today's Dow is an average of 30 stocks, most of which have nothing to do with traditional heavy industry.

Henry Ford built the Ford Quadricycle, the first Ford vehicle ever developed.

John Philip Sousa composed "The Stars and Stripes Forever."

Famous people born in 1896 include U.S. Senator Everett Dirksen from Illinois; actor George Burns; Bessie Wallis Warfield (later the Duchess of Windsor, the woman for whom King Edward VIII of the United Kingdom abdicated his throne); First Lady Mamie Eisenhower; author F. Scott Fitzgerald; Stafford L. Warren, the inventor of the mammogram; and Percy Spencer, the inventor of the microwave oven.

Famous people who died in 1896 include pioneering Civil War photographer Mathew B. Brady; author and abolitionist Harriet Beecher Stowe, best known for *Uncle Tom's Cabin*; and George Washington Gale Ferris Jr., inventor of the Ferris wheel.

Welcome to Ottumwa 1896

Woman Was In His Power.

MARSHALLTOWN, Ia., Oct. 22.—E. G. Bowman, the alleged bigamist, was bound over to the grand jury, and in default of $500 bail went to jail. The woman whom he lived with here now admits that they were never married, and says she has been completely in Bowman's power, though conscious she was doing illegal and wrongful acts.

Suicide at Libertyville.

Fairfield, Ia., July 21.—(Special.)—James Vance Blair, residing at Libertyville, who has been in ill health for a long number of years, attempted to commit suicide last evening. He had not been feeling as well as common and started for the barn, where the family found him a short time after, bleeding profusely from a pistol shot at the base of the head. Doctors were immediately sent for, but the man was unconscious ever since and it is reported that he can not survive his injuries. None of the family knew that there was a pistol about the house, as he had one last winter but it was lost, but since he has committed the deed, it was found that he had borrowed one from his brother-in-law a short time ago.

Norms in reporting were far different in 1896, with suicides described in gory detail and stories about "murders" published even before the victims had died.

Double Missouri Murder.

WEST LIBERTY, Oct. 27.—Mormon elders have been holding meetings in Elliott county, and Elit Isom and his family joined the church. Friday night three young men named Sparks declared that they would break up the Mormon meeting, and started out to do so. They stopped at the home of Bill Isom, and on being refused they fired through the doors and windows. Elit Isom was shot twice in the breast, and Mrs. Isom was shot in the abdomen. The injuries to both are considered fatal.

Aged Couple Murdered by Burglars.

SHAMOKIN, Pa., Oct. 27.—At a cost of probably two lives, four masked robbers stole $5,000 from Mr. and Mrs. Anthony Monaghan in the mining village of Rappahannock, one mile from Girardville. The heads of Mr. and Mrs. Monaghan were crushed with sandbags. They are in a critical condition. Parties of men are scouring the mountains on each side of the village in search of the robbers. The Monaghans are the owners of the Rappahannock hotel. The burglars gained entrance by climbing on the porch, forcing the second story shutters with jimmies and then making their way to the room where the old couple slept. There the assault was made and the money secured.

HUNG A NEGRO.

And Five Others are in Danger of Similar Treatment.

Little Rock, Ark., July 18.—A passenger from Malvern, states that six negroes were arrested charged with setting fire to the town. The people are greatly excited One negro has already been strung up and there is hardly any doubt that the entire six will be summarily dealt with by the indignant citizens. No confirmation of the report is obtainable on account of lack of telegraph or telephone connection.

Little Rock, Ark., July 18.—Sheriff Fitzhugh, of Hot Springs county, tonight brought to the penitentiary Eugene Iggreham. D. Miller and Cash Williams, three men arrested at Malvern on charge of setting fire to town last night. The sheriff says no negro was lynched, He had trouble in getting the prisoners on the train as the crowd was anxious to get possession of them. Williams who confesses complicity in the crime, implicating two white men, says it was done for plundder.

Jim Crow laws enforcing racial segregation were in full swing across the nation, particularly in the South, in 1896. It is not known which of the two versions of this story -- published together in the same edition of the newspaper -- is actually correct.

At the time of the Encampment, the start of the Spanish-American War was still more than 18 months in the future, but tensions were already on the rise.

The Cuban War of Independence, one of several conflicts fought by Cubans throughout the 19th century in seeking freedom from Spain, had been underway since 1895. In the Philippines, the revolution began in August 1896, just as the Encampment was ending.

Some American newspapers agitated for U.S. intervention, and public opinion was widely in support of the Cubans. When rioting broke out in Cuba, the battleship *USS Maine* was sent to Havana. In February, 1898, *Maine* exploded in Havana harbor, killing 260 of the approximately 400 crewmen. Though the cause of the explosion is still unclear more than a century later, a wave of public indignation, fanned by partisan newspapers, led to sending U.S. troops (including Iowa's National Guard regiments) to Cuba to end the civil war. Spain responded by severing diplomatic relations with the United States.

The war lasted ten weeks and was fought in both the Caribbean and the Pacific, ostensibly in support of both the Cuban and Philippine revolts.

After losing the Philippines and facing the certain loss of Cuba, Spain opted for peace in July 1898, relinquishing all claims of sovereignty over Cuba and the Philippines.

The war ended with an independent Cuba and with the United States in possession of the Philippine Islands, Guam, and Puerto Rico. The Philippines became an independent nation in 1946.

TWO BATTLES IN CUBA.

General Munoz, According to Official Reports, Forces Maceo From His Stronghold—Defeated a Second Time By the Garrison at Artemisa.

JACKSONVILLE, Oct. 24.—On the hurricane deck of the filibustering steamer Dauntless is a great stain that was made by the life blood of one of the vessel's crew, killed by a shot from the Spanish gunboat Contramastra during the filibuster's last voyage. On the morning of Oct. 18 the steamer was leaving a point on the northern coast of the province of Pinar del Rio, after having landed her third cargo of supplies for the insurgents. When 10 miles from the shore the Contramastre bore down upon them and the Dauntless was forced to her best speed. Shot after shot was fired by the Spaniards. The little vessel was gaining, when a cry from the pilothouse and the crash of wood indicated that one shot had struck. Captain Lomm rushed forward and found that Henry Wilkerson, a member of the crew, had been struck and cut in two. Driving ahead at full speed, the Dauntless finally got out of range and escaped the Spaniard.

PHILIPPINE REBELLION

Revolt Against the Spanish Is Spreading In the Islands.

HORROR ENACTED IN CAVITE

Atrocities Perpetrated by the Rebels—Inmates of a Monastery Tortured to Death—Great Damage Done to Property.

VANCOUVER, B. C., Oct. 22.—The Empress of Japan, which has just arrived from the orient, brings advices regarding the rebellion against the Spanish in the Philippine islands, confirming the previous reports that the Spaniards will likely have another war as serious as that in Cuba on their hands. Governor General Blanco realizes that with the present force he is unable to quell the revolt, and consequently is awaiting the arrival of reinforcements before striking a decisive blow. Meantime the rebels are doing a great deal of damage to the property and murdering and robbing the inhabitants. The rebellion has spread to the provinces of Manilla, Bulacan, Pampanga, Nueva, Tarlac, La Laguina, Cavite and Batangas. An illustration of the atrocities perpetrated by the rebels is furnished by an attack on a large monastery in Cavite province, which they have since used as their headquarters. This was one of the first places attacked. Maddened by the refusal of the padreas to yield, the rebels on getting inside resorted to the most fiendish tortures in order to wreak vengeance on the padreas. Several of them were hanged to trees and roasted to death by burning kerosene oil. Others were put to death in an even more cruel manner, portions of their bodies being cut off by piece-meal. In the monastery the rebels were well supplied with rifles, ammunition and food and so far have succeeded in driving off the Spanish troops.

Situation at Manilla.

In Manilla things are practically at a standstill. The prisons are crowded with prisoners and over 300 have been deported to the Carolines. By torture the Spaniards have wrung many secrets from the prisoners. A triangular mark cut in the arm is the badge of membership of the revolutionary party. The prison at Manilla, which has earned for itself the title of "black hole of Manilla," is an old fortress. Prisoners are thrown into a dungeon, entrance into which is gained by a hole in the roof. The only ventilation is through a barred opening underneath the platform floor, and at high tide this means of ventilation is totally closed and large numbers of prisoners who did not die from suffocation were found to have torn each other in a dreadful manner in fits of insanity. Numerous accusations of cowardice have been made against the Spanish. In a brush with the rebels they placed native troops in the van and when these were dispersed, the Spaniards fled.

Rebellion In Formosa.

Further advices from Formosa state that the Japanese are pacifying that island by exterminating the natives. Men, women and children are bayoneted by Japanese troops, while the whole country is overrun by bandits. In many districts there has been severe drouth, and in addition to the horrors, famine stares the people in the face. A traveler who has just returned from a tour through the "camphor" district denies that the rebellion has been suppressed, although the villages were deserted and everywhere was evidence of destruction caused by fire and sword.

Once again it is announced that the Mohammedan rebellion has been suppressed, although missionary reports do not in any way agree with official intelligence. Meanwhile there is a lively rising in Chung Lok district, about 100 miles from Swatow islands. This is the district where Hahkkes destroyed the property of the Basel missions, for which act the German government obtained ample reparation. So far no missions stations are reported as being in danger, and troops have been dispatched to the scene.

Welcome to Ottumwa 1896

SULTAN IN UGLY MOOD

Arming of Mussulmans May Mean Renewal of Massacres.

CHRISTIANS IN DIRE PERIL.

Everything Points to Further Trouble In Turkey—Great Apprehension Exists In Armenia—Death of M. Challemel-Lacour—Foreign News.

(Copyrighted, 1896, by Associated Press.)
CONSTANTINOPLE, Oct. 26.—The report that trouble of a serious nature is brewing here has so often been sent out that any fresh announcement to that effect is looked upon as having little or no foundation in fact. But in spite of this it is but right to state once more that everything points to further and very serious trouble preparing on all sides throughout the Turkish empire. The ball was set rolling on Wednesday last when the sultan signed two irades which were issued the next day levying a poll tax of five piasters per head on all Mussulmans and increasing the taxes on sheep, public works and education by 1 to 2½ per cent, the funds so raised to be devoted to military purposes.

This caused the representatives of the powers to send a collective note to the porte, couched in the strongest language, calling attention to the danger that the arming of the Mussulmans was certain to create, and pointing out generally the critical situation of affairs in the Turkish empire. But large purchases of arms have already been made, and the danger increases hourly. The porte today sent a reply to the collective note of the ambassadors. As usual, however, it was an evasive answer, and in substance simply stated that the money derived from the additional taxes was only intended to complete the armament of the Mustahfuz, or Landstrum, the third and last class of the Turkish army reserves, and to strengthen the armament of the other land forces of the sultan.

The action of the Turkish government in completing the armament of the Mustahfuz indicates that the emperor is facing a situation which may necessitate calling forth all the military forces at his disposal, and it indicates that the situation is the gravest since the Russo-Turkish war. Under these circumstances it is but natural that considerable uneasiness prevails. Of course, there is always in view the probability at least that the sultan by these movements is simply seeking to detract at-

FATAL ENDING OF A BULL FIGHT.

Mexican Picador Impaled on a Maddened Animal's Horns.

NOGALES, Oct. 27.—A bull fight with fatal results occurred at Nogales, Sonora, Mex., and for a short time caused a panic in the audience. One of the bulls, becoming more enraged than usual at these rather tame fights, ranted about the arena, goring everything within its reach. A horse was disemboweled, and a picador, Jose Angulo, in an attempt to place a thorn on the side of the wild animal, was caught on one of its long horns, which pierced him like a sword. He was tossed and fell to the ground, bleeding and mangled, where the beast held him between his horns and pawed at him. He was frightfully injured, and died a few moments later.

Princess Helene's State Entry Into Rome.
ROME, Oct. 23.—Princess Helene of Montenegro made her state entry into Rome today. Her relatives arrived here at 11 o'clock and were welcomed by King Humbert, Queen Marguerite, the crown prince, the ministers, members of the diplomatic corps, etc. The streets from the railway station to the palace were thronged with crowds of people, lined with troops and gaily decorated. The procession, composed of 20 royal carriages, was preceded and followed by strong detachments of cuirassiers. Their majesties and the princess were continually cheered by the crowds. Military bands stationed at intervals along the route played the national anthems of Italy and Montenegro.

Deadly Grade Crossing.

NEW YORK, Oct. 27.—Dr. W. W. Palmer and Miss Fannie Palmer, his granddaughter, 15 years of age, of Keansburg, N. J., were killed today and William Hauran of Atlantic City was probably fatally injured by a train of the Central railroad of New Jersey at Keansburg. Mr. Hauran had gone to Keansburg to visit the Palmers and all three, with a daughter of Dr. Palmer, were in a carriage crossing the railroad track when a train that had been unobserved by them, struck the vehicle, wrecking it. Dr. and Miss Palmer were killed instantly. Hauran can scarcely survive his injuries. Dr. Palmer's daughter was not seriously hurt.

Sensational Shooting Affray.

KNOXVILLE, Tenn., Oct. 27.—A special from Coal Creek, the famous rioting mining town, 30 miles from here, says a very sensational shooting affray occurred there last night in which two men were killed and another wounded. The fight occurred at a McKinley and Hobart meeting. A negro named Bud Black began shooting at another negro named Frank Martin. They exchanged several shots and Martin fell mortally wounded with two bullet holes through his body. One of the shots struck and instantly killed Squire Robert Laughlin, a justice of the peace and one of the leading citizens of the town. Others were hit but not seriously hurt. Black made his escape.

A DISASTROUS WRECK

Two Engines Completely Demolished and a Mail Car Shattered.

TWO MEN WERE KILLED

And Ten More Badly Hurt—All of the Injured were Train Men—Engineer and Mail Agent Killed in the Collision.

NO PASSENGERS WERE INJURED.

The Wreck Occurred on the Illinois Central.

Clinton, Ill., Aug. 1.—A disastrous wreck occurred on the Illinois Central here today. Both engines were completely wrecked. The mail car was shattered into splinters. The other mail and baggage cars were badly damaged. Engineer Chas. Burchnaugh and William Baker were killed. Ten trainmen were injured. No passengers were hurt.

Welcome to Ottumwa 1896

A HORRIFYING CATASTROPHE

Frightful Railroad Collision Yesterday Afternoon at Atlantic City.

ONE HUNDRED WERE KILLED

A Reading Express Train Ran Broadside into an Excursion Train.

The Details of the Awful Affair Cannot Be Fully Told at Present.

Atlantic City, N. J., July 30.—A railroad accident, horrible in its details and sickening in its results, occurred this evening just outside the city and as a result about one hundred persons were either killed or injured. The Reading railroad express which left Philadelphia at 5:40 this evening for Atlantic City, crashed into the Pennsylvania railroad excursion excursion train at second signal tower, four miles out from here. The Pennsylvania train was returning from Bridgeton with a party of excursionists from that place, Millville and surrounding towns. It was loaded with passengers, and a rough estimate of the killed and injured is placed at one hundred.

At second signal tower the tracks of the two roads cross. The Reading train was given the signal but it either failed to work or the speed of the express was too great to be checked in time. It caught the excursion train broadside and plunged through it, literally clearing the tracks. The engine of the Reading road was spattered with blood. Every car was jammed to its fullest capacity. As soon as the news reached Atlantic City relief trains were dispatched to the scene with cots and surgeons. As quick as the bodies were recovered they were carried into local hospitals and undertakers' shops. A general fire alarm was sounded and the departments promptly responded, aided in digging for the victims. The first relief train bore into the city twenty-seven mangled corpses of men, women and children. The next train carried fifteen maimed and wounded

the crash and were utterly demolished. What remained of the third car was tumbled into the ditch at the road side.

Responsibility for the accident cannot now be fixed. Charles C. Rynick, of Bridgeton, who was in one of the rear cars of the excursion train, said: "Crash came almost before we knew it. Third car was cut right in two and lower portion of it lifted bodily from the track and tumbled over. Every car was crowded and it is horrible to think of the numbers who must be lying under those ruins. The roof of one car fell in and everybody in that car was buried under it. I think there must have been fully eighty or one hundred killed."

Rescuers went to work. Axes and shovels were plied with the greatest vigor, and at almost every half dozen strokes a mangled form was brought up and laid tenderly on the waiting pallets. A bent, blood-stained member was turned aside by a rescuer, who brought to sight a woman's arm. It had been wrenched off almost by the roots and nothing remained but the dripping stump. Even the hand was gone. Not five minutes later a chance blow from a pick revealed the still more ghastly remnant, a human heart, that only a few short hours before had been throbbing with life. Scattered about the ground near the wreck were many pieces of clothing which had been torn from the victims.

THE OPERATOR ARRESTED
Wm. Thurlow, the operator in the

On July 30, 1896, just as the Encampment in Ottumwa was winding down, one of the nation's largest and deadliest railroad crashes occurred in Atlantic City, New Jersey, when a Reading Railroad express train plowed into an excursion train carrying members of a lodge group. About 50 passengers and crew were killed. A few minutes after the collision, the boiler of the Reading steam locomotive exploded, spraying scalding water over already-injured passengers. The collision was blamed on Reading Railroad engineer Edward Farr, who died in the collision. (His wife died of apparent shock upon being told of the accident.)

Though the Atlantic City wreck was one of the worst, railroad collisions, derailments, and other accidents were not uncommon during the era.

Engineer Edward Farr, who died with his hand on the throttle, was taken out early this morning. It was with much difficulty that his rigid fingers were unclasped from the lever. His eyes looked skyward with ghastly glare. He had been pinned down by the chest and apparently met instant death. Almost every bone in the body of one man was broken when he was taken from the ruins. Many were so frightfully mangled as to be beyond recognition.

DEBRIS CLEARED AWAY.
By eight o'clock this morning the

DEATH ON THE RAIL.

Further Particulars of the Wreck at Atlantic City.

DEATH LIST IS LARGE.

Many Killed Outright and Many More Terribly Injured—it is not Known Yet Where the Responsibility Lies.

MANY SAD AND SICKENING SIGHTS

The Responsibility for the Wreck not yet Determined.

Atlantic City, N. J., July 31.—The midsummer sun burst this morning upon a sleepless, horror stricken community. The gaiety which will mark this resort from now until the end of the season will be but a faint echo of the days past. A death pall has fallen upon it. On every street corner and hotel piazzi trembling lips discuss last night's fearful catastrophe and await additional details.

The list of dead revised number forty-two and this is thought to be correct, although possibly more bodies are under the debris in the pond beside the wreck. The injured so far as known aggregate forty-three. The force of rescuers continued at work throughout the night but no more bodies were found.

Engineer Edward Farr, who died with his hand on the throttle, was taken out early this morning. It was with came into the depot and stopped, the sight of the survivors in the four rear coaches who had been in the wrecked train was pitiful.

Persons were to be seen reclining on the seats with bandages about their heads, from which, in some instances, blood was trickling. Two little boys and girls had deep wounds on their faces and their clothing was nearly all spattered with blood.

Two sisters, Nettie and Julia Pierce, were badly injured. Julia had a bandage around her head which concealed the ragged wound that the physicians found necessary to close with several stitches. She said she had been knocked against the seat in front of her and rendered unconscious.

Her sister had a swollen nose and her eyes were discolored.

In one of the seats sat S. D. Frasier and wife, their ten-month's-old daughter, Alice and two boys. The heads of all but Alice had been cut and were stitched and bandaged. Baby Alice, at the time of the collision, was asleep in the lap of her mother and when all were thrown into a heap she fell under the seat and escaped without a bruise.

Among the survivors were Mrs. Mary Kiger, of Elmira, N. J., whose head was badly cut and whose back was injured. When the crash came she was sitting in the seat opposite her husband and looking across the meadows. There was a shadow, she said, then the awful crash came, and amid wild shrieks the car was upset and I knew no more.

Mr. Kiger succeeded in carrying his wife out somehow or other in the wild rush which followed.

In the same car was little Reba Bowers, 7 years old, of Bridgetown, eating candy when the collison came. She was pitched head first under the opposite seat and had her back badly cut. Opposite her sat Mrs. John Roons with her husband. As the car went over, Roons raised the window and shoved her through it feet first just as the seat

Welcome to Ottumwa 1896

The Second Regiment
Iowa National Guard

The roots of the Iowa National Guard were set down in 1838 when Iowa was still a territory and the territorial legislature concluded that a militia was needed. The Iowa Militia was first mobilized in late 1839 to take action against Missouri, after disputes about the location of the boundary line between the two states led to a conflict still known as the Honey War. Missouri had tried to collect taxes in the disputed area, and Missouri officials were ejected by the sheriff of Van Buren County. Both states called out their militias, including more than a thousand Iowans, but ultimately it was decided to leave the question of boundaries to the U.S. Congress. Ultimately, the border was drawn by the Supreme Court.

Company G, Second Regiment Iowa National Guard, in about 1986, posed in front of the nearly-new Wapello County Courthouse.

134

Second Regiment Iowa National Guard

The militia also was called out in response to the Spirit Lake Massacre of 1857, patrolling to prevent further raids. This led, during the Civil War, to the formation of the Northern Border Brigade, intended to protect settlers from Native Americans after federal troops were pulled away from the frontier to fight in the war.

A Southern Border Brigade defended Iowa's southern tiers of counties from Confederate irregulars who executed cross-border raids. In October 1864, Confederate irregulars dressed in federal uniforms crossed into Davis County, robbed a number of farms, took hostages, and killed two Union veterans.

At the end of the Civil War, the Iowa State Militia reverted to being a collection of independent, volunteer organizations. In 1876 the Militia was reorganized into regiments, and in 1877 the Militia was renamed the Iowa National Guard.

An 1877 report points out that no financial aid of any kind was granted to the militia by the state government. The officers and men paid for their own uniforms, ammunition, armory rental, and contingent expenses.

In 1893 the existing units were reorganized into two brigades of two regiments each.

The companies comprising the Second Regiment served in various capacities, from protecting prisoners threatened by mobs, to protecting railroad property, to preventing violence by striking miners, to marching off to serve in the Spanish-American War and in World War I and beyond.

Company G, the portion of the Second Regiment based in Ottumwa, was involved in the dedication of the World's Columbian Exposition in Chicago in 1892, the inauguration of Iowa Governor Bois in 1890, and at Muchakinock (Mahaska County) in 1894 when striking coal miners threatened violence.

At the time of the encampment, the Second Regiment was composed of twelve companies, based in Keokuk, Davenport, Washington, Centerville, Ft. Madison, Ottumwa, Chariton, Iowa City, Grinnell, Newton, Muscatine, and Tipton.

With the outbreak of the Spanish-American War, the entire Iowa National Guard was mobilized into federal service on May 17, 1898. The four guard regiments were renumbered to follow in numerical sequence the 48 regiments which had been provided by Iowa during the Civil War. The Second Regiment thus became the 50th Regiment. The 50th was sent for training to Jacksonville, Florida. During service in the Spanish-American War, the 50th lost 32 men to non-battle losses, primarily typhoid fever. Company G lost two men, both to typhoid.

The 50th was mustered out of federal service on November 30, 1899.

Welcome to Ottumwa 1896

Company G's original armory was located in the building at left, which had been built as the Methodist Episcopal Church. The building at right was the county courthouse. Both of these buildings were removed so the current Wapello County Courthouse could be built on the site. The new courthouse was dedicated in 1894.

Company G, from
Eads' *Illustrated History of Ottumwa*, 1885

"The notation of a military company under the head of amusements may be somewhat out of place, and yet Co. G., 2d Regiment, I. N. G., is an organization that will probably figure more largely in the social sphere than on the field of battle. It is composed of the best young men of the city and is a leading social organization. It is quite probable, too, that the courage that is displayed by the boys in facing the perilous battery of bright smiles at their society events, is of the same order that would march them, with light step into the volcanic mouth of cannon.

This company was organized in the spring of 1884 and the first officers elected were: Howard Hedrick, Captain; W.C. Wyman, First Lieut., C.K. Blake, Second Lieut. Shortly after the organization, Capt. Hedrick resigned and was succeeded by W. A. McGrew. Capt. McGrew is fast bringing the boys to the front in the matter of discipline and drill and much is expected of them. Their Armory is located on Fourth street, adjoining the Court House."

Second Regiment Iowa National Guard

Company G
in the Spanish-American War
(Listed by Capt. S. B. Evans in
History of Wapello County, Iowa and Representative Citizens, 1901)

The following list of personnel of Company G, 50th Iowa Infantry, served in the Spanish-American War.

The company was mustered into the United States service at Des Moines, Iowa, on May 17, 1898. It left the state May 21, 1898, and was stationed at Jacksonville, Florida. It was mustered out of service on November 30, 1899.

Capt. F. W. Eckers
First Lieut. Theodore A. Stoessel
Second Lieut. Charles S. Tindell
Sergt. William R. Armstrong
Sergt., Q.M. Maurice G. Holt
Sergt. Alexander T. Kasparson
Sergt. William D. Sumner
Sergt. Leroy Christie
Sergt. Alvin J. Crail
Corp. Roy J. Cook
Corp. Albert V. Lindell
Corp. Eugene B. Hill, Jr.
Corp. Charles Brown
Corp. William F. Bickley
Corp. Edward Steller
Corp. Grant Irving Emery
Corp. Samuel Manro
Corp. George H. Elliott
Corp. Mernie S. Ballagh
Corp. John H. Wright
Musician Joseph Hayes, died at Jacksonville, Florida, September 8, 1898 (typhoid)
Musician Otto Armstrong
Artificer* William T. Smith
Wagoner Ivory H. Cook

(continued on page 139)

* An artificer is a member of an armed-forces service
who is skilled at working on mechanical devices

Welcome to Ottumwa 1896

Ottumwa soldiers of Company G, Iowa National Guard, aboard a train at the Wabash depot on May 17, 1898. The troops were en route to Des Moines where they were mustered into federal service. They were then sent on to Jacksonville, Florida, where they served during the Spanish-American War.
The Wabash depot was located near the end of the railroad bridge leading to Dain Manufacturing (John Deere Ottumwa Works). The bridge is now part of the trail system.

Second Regiment Iowa National Guard
(continued from page 137)

Barnum, Emerson E.
Boughner, Charles S.
Bowser, John W.
Curran, John
Church, Dean K.
Cullen, Frank
Davis, Harvey A.
DeValt, Albert
Ellis, Foster R.
Ellis, Macy M.
Emery, Roscoe
Frost, Robert
Graves, Chauncey A.
Grube, Oscar A. died at Des Moines, October 6, 1898 (typhoid)
Higgins, Bert D.
Hobbs, William A.
Hobbs, William P.
Hedrick, Eugene F.
Langford, J. Elliott
Lowe, Robert W.
Mitchell, Mark M. H.
Mungoven, Thomas
Moore, Charles F.
Moore, Charles E.
Parker, Alva A.
Parker, Fred W.
Pickett, Charles S.
Rolison, Merit V.
Riordan, John T.
Riordan, Allen B.
Scott, Charles U.
Simmons, Harry M.
Smith, Edward O.
Sunley, Nate L.
Snyder, John J.
Trease, John C.
Trowbridge, Edward A.
Terrell, Otis T.
Wheelock, Herbert K.
Williams, William W.

Welcome to Ottumwa 1896

SIXTEEN YEARS AGO TODAY, OTTUMWA'S CO. G LEFT HERE FOR THE EUROPEAN BATTLEFRONT; G. A. R. HONOR GUARD ESCORTED MEN TO TRAIN

O. B. NELSON
2nd Lieutenant

F. B. YOUNKIN
1st Lieutenant

EDWARD STELLER
Captain

PHILLIP BINKS
1st Sergeant

Luneville
—:o:—
Baccarat
—:o:—
Champagne
—:o:—
Chateau Thierry
—:o:—
The Ourcq
—:o:—
St. Mihiel
—:o:—
Argonne-Meuse
—:o:—
Sedan
—:o:—
Army of the Rhine

The commissioned officers and the first sergeant of the 153 men of Co. G, 168th Infantry, 42nd. division, who marched away from Ottumwa to the battlefields of the World war sixteen years ago, are shown in this group of pictures. Steller returned from the war with the commission of major. Nelson was promoted to a captaincy and commanded Co. H of Oskaloosa at the time of his death. Younkin was also promoted to a captaincy and commanded Co. G in most of its engagements. The war strength of the company was twenty-three officers. One hundred men of Co. G were entitled to the Purple Heart decoration which was revived by the government last year in connection with the Washington bicentennial.

Sixteen years ago today Ottumwa's Company G of the old Third the British steamship Baltic and proceeded to the harbor at Hali- cited for the distinguished service cross.

Second Regiment Iowa National Guard

Company G in the First World War
(Thursday, August 17, 1933 *Courier* story)

*In 1933, the Ottumwa Courier ran this story reflecting on
the service of Company G in the World War.*

Sixteen years ago today *[i.e., August 17, 1917]* Ottumwa's Company G of the old Third Iowa infantry departed from Ottumwa on the "great adventure." The trail it followed led to the battlefields of France in the greatest of all wars. Today those Ottumwa members of the unit rolled back the curtain of time to reminisce on those stirring times with their tragedy and glory.

Reference is made to the company as a part of the old Third Iowa, as a matter of fact, it was assigned a place in the 168th infantry as a part of the Forty-second division before it left Ottumwa. However, the company that served in France was a direct descendant of the famous Third Iowa, which had participated in other campaigns which preceded the great war.

The night before the departure from Ottumwa, the soldiers, who had been in camp at Camp Andrew from July 2, were allowed to spend the night at home. Camp Andrew was located on a field on the North Court road across from what is now the Dr. F. L. Nelson home. *[The 1933 city directory lists Dr. Frederick L. Nelson's home address as "Seven Acres", a property which was located at North Court Road and Elmdale. The property was used as an officers' club during World War II, as a studio by KBIZ Radio, and as a summer camp. It is the present-day site of North Hy-Vee. The area across North Court Road, once Camp Andrew, is occupied by housing.]* Some who spent that night at home counted it as their last with their families.

At 6:45 the morning of August 17 the company assembled in the armory, corner of Market and Second streets *[The 1917 city directory lists the armory at 133 N. Market, which would be closer to the intersection of Market and Third]*, for the march to the train which waited at the Union station. An excerpt from The Courier's news story of the departure *[that is, from August 1917]* follows.

"Ottumwa has sent soldiers to other wars in other years, and on occasions the departure of troops has been marked by more elaborate ceremony than attended the entraining of the company today. But never was there a more impressive farewell. The look of grim determination that the soldiers wore was reflected in the countenances of the men and women who watched them. The holiday spirit was missing and in its place was a realization that with the departure of Ottumwa's 153 infantrymen, the whole city becomes a participant in the war which is to decide the fate of civilization."

Welcome to Ottumwa 1896

Local veterans of the Civil war served as a guard of honor for Company G in a parade that led through the downtown streets. Two bands were in the parade -- one a hastily organized local band, the other being a part of the Brundage carnival which was showing in Ottumwa at that time. The First Cavalry band, with Ottumwa its local headquarters, was then in camp at Grinnell. The late T.J. Phillips, city commissioner and band enthusiast, served as drum major in the parade. As the procession passed the Ottumwa Gas Co. *[located at 104 W. Main]* a large flag was unfurled and from its folds flowers showered down upon the marching men. At 7:10 the train steamed out of the station bearing the Ottumwans on the first leg of their long journey.

The first camp of G company away from home was at the state fair grounds at Des Moines. There the men remained until September 9 when they were sent to Camp Mills, N.Y., arriving September 14. On October 18 the Ottumwans boarded the USS Grant, a converted German boat, and steamed away with a convoy bound for the shores of France. The boat bearing the local unit, however, developed boiler trouble, and put back into port. On October 27 the men encamped on Governor's Island at Fort Jay where they remained until November 22 when they boarded the British steamship Baltic at Halifax, Nova Scotia. The harbor was reached November 24 and the Baltic left the following day with a convoy for England. The landing was made at Liverpool on December 8 and entrained for Winchester. Reaching Winchester Co. G camped for two days. The crossing of the British channel was made the night of December 11. On December 12, nearly four months after the departure from the Union station at Ottumwa, the infantrymen set foot on French soil, at Le Havre.

Following, in brief, is the log of G Co. following the unloading at Le Havre:

December 15, entrained for Ft. De Peigney and arrived there the same day. From Ft. De Peigney the unit was moved to St. Ceirgues and left for the front about February 23, 1918. March 6 to 11, first hitch in the trenches. March 6 to June 19, on Lorraine front. July 4 to July 19, engaged in Champagne defense. July 25 to August 3, engaged in Argone [sic]-Meuse offensive. September 12 to 16, engaged in St. Mihiel offensive. September 17 to 30, engaged in the Essey and Pannes sector. October 13 to 31, engaged in Argonne-Meuse offensive. November 5 to 9, march on Sedan. December 15 to April 2, 1919 in army of occupation.

The famous 42nd or Rainbow division of Co. G was a unit [that] saw 110 days service in the front lines, which was the longest stretch of any of the divisions in the

Second Regiment Iowa National Guard

American Expeditionary Forces. March 16, 1919, final review by Gen. John Pershing. April 8, left Germany for Brest, France. April 17, Leviathan, carrying unit, left France. April 26, landed at New York City. May 17, arrived at Ottumwa.

The 42nd division had a total of 13,919 casualties and captured 1,317 prisoners. In the division 243 were cited for the distinguished service cross.

Of the men who marched to the Union station here sixteen years ago, these were killed or died overseas:

Capt. O. B. Nelson*, Carl Gillen, Harry Arnold, LeRoy Dailey, David Davis, George Duffield, Earl Dunham, Ralph Grammer, Carl Hilgardner, William Lindsay, William E. J. Maloney, Patrick Shuckrow. Lindsay, a private, was the first to die. He was hit at Lorraine. Davis, a Hedrick boy, died in the Champagne. The toll of life at Chateau Thierry included Arnold [,] Dailey, Duffield, Maloney, Grammar [sic], Hilgardner and Gillen. Captain Nelson and Dunham died at St. Mihiel and Shuckrow during the occupation of the Rhine. Walter B. Schaefer**, another Ottumwan who joined the unit after it left Ottumwa, was also killed overseas.

Only fifteen of the 153 who marched away from here went unscathed through the various battles and were neither gassed or wounded. Capt. Edward Steller was the first to be hit and retired from the front at Lorraine. He was later promoted to major and had charge of a prison camp.

Those Ottumwa members of the company who have died since returning from service overseas *[i.e., between 1919 and 1933]* follow: Capt. F. B. Younkin, Clarence Fiedler, Dewey Alderdice, Thomas Barkwell, Arthur Goehring, Merle Martin, Earl McCoy, Maurice Proctor, Cecil Simmer and John Wilt.

The company's full strength was 606 men and at one time the unit numbered men from practically every state in the union. There were twenty-three officers. The total number who were killed or died was forty-three. The unit took thirty-three prisoners and captured eighteen of the enemy's weapons.

[Information included within brackets and in italics has been added to the quoted material in order to provide context and bring the 1933 article up to date.]

* Ottumwa's American Legion post is named for Capt. Nelson.

** Ottumwa's Veteran's of Foreign Wars post and the Ottumwa School District's stadium are named for Walter B. Schaefer (though there is often confusion about the correct spelling)

Sources

Baker, Chris. *In Retrospect.* Donning Company, Virginia Beach VA, 1992.

Chronicling America website
https://chroniclingamerica.loc.gov

Evans, Capt. S. B. *History of Wapello County, Iowa, and Representative Citizens.* Biographical Publishing Company, Chicago IL, 1901.

Hansen, Bill. Personal conversation.

Iowa National Guard website
https://www.iowanationalguard.com/History/History/Pages/Home.aspx

Lemberger, Michael W. and Wilson J. Warren. *Ottumwa.* Images of America, Arcadia Publishing, Chicago IL, 2006.

Lemberger, Michael W. and Leigh Michaels. *Ottumwa.* Postcard History Series, Arcadia Publishing, Chicago IL, 2007.

Michaels, Leigh. *Movers & Shakers.* PBL Limited, Ottumwa IA, 2018.

Naumann, Molly Myers. Personal conversation.

Parrish, Sue. *Days Gone By.* PBL Limited, Ottumwa IA, 2007.

Potter, Doug and Leigh Michaels. *Fire!* PBL Limited, Ottumwa IA, 2017.

Waterman, H.L. *History of Wapello County, Iowa.* S. J. Clarke Publishing Company, Chicago IL, 1914.

About the Editor

Leigh Michaels (www.leighmichaels.com) is the author of more than 100 books, including contemporary and historical romance novels, non-fiction works about writing, and local history.

More than 35 million copies of her books have been published in 27 languages and 120 countries. Six of her books were finalists in the annual RITA competition for best romance novel, sponsored by the Romance Writers of America. She teaches romance writing online at Gotham Writers Workshop.

She owns and operates PBL Limited (www.pbllimited.com), a publisher of niche-market non-fiction, based in Ottumwa, Iowa.

For more information about these and other books, calendars and products, visit
www.pbllimited.com
PBL Limited
P.O. Box 935
Ottumwa Iowa 52501